What People Have to Say About *Joyfinity*

"Discover how to master your energy by choosing the tool of being in tune or harmonized with the energy of Hummingbird. Joy is surely induced by this method. Wow. I so want to read more. A magnificent shift for me. I feel blessed to read your work."

—Toni Ann Mazza,
Creator of Magnificent Life Changes

"I remember sitting in Ojai, with Tricia, watching her create joy out of the invisible energies of the Universe. She's included this energy weaving in her new book, *Joyfinity*! My personal favorite sections are those on Sacred Technologies for playing with energy. Thanks, Tricia, for opening our hearts and eyes to what's possible."

—Eve-Marie Devaliere,
creator of Own Your Frequency

"Who knew that learning about the essence of joy and how to implement it could be both practical and exhilarating at the same time! I love how each chapter lays out the differences of how each element of energy is constructed in a thorough, yet minimalistic, style. It's like going to a sumptuous smorgasbord with an unending array of delicious food to eat. The possibilities of all the different combinations of ideas within this book that you could apply and cavort with are infinite. Try as you might, you will never be able to use them all in this lifetime. This is a book you will love to revisit over and over, on the one hand for the goldmine of ideas you can use to live a more fulfilling and joyful life and on the other hand for the sheer pleasure of reading it."

—**Susan James**,
author, speaker, and creator
of Making Peace Action Program

Joyfinity

Joyfinity
the WOW of energy mastery

Tricia Jeane Croyle

Copyright © 2021 by Tricia Jeane Croyle

All rights are reserved. No part of this book may be reproduced either by any mechanical, photographic, or electronic process, or in the form of a sound recording. Nor may it be stored in a retrieval system, or otherwise transmitted for public or private use.

The author of this book does not dispense medical advice nor prescribe any technique as a form of treatment for physical, emotional, or medical problems. The intent of the author is to offer information of a general nature to help the reader in his quest for emotional and spiritual wellbeing. In the event the reader uses any of the information in this book for himself, the author assumes no responsibility for his actions.

ISBN 13: 978-1-7330509-4-4
ISBN 10:1-7330509-4-9

Book Interior and E-book Design by Amit Dey | amitdey2528@gmail.com

Other Creations by Tricia Jeane Croyle

Books

From Heartache to Joy: One Woman's Journey Home

From Heartache to Joy: A Companion Playbook

Beyond Joy: A Journey into Freedom, Wisdom, Power, and Wellbeing

Absolute Joy: A Journey Beyond Time to Nowhere

Cards

The Morning Prayer Cards

The Rose Path Meditation Cards

Absolute Joy Rose Path Meditation cards

Free Gift

Get a free gift for joining The Joy Project at www.tricia-jeanecroyle.com

Contents

Acknowledgments xiv
Preface. xv
    The Joy Project xvii
    The Joy Series. xviii
    The Energy Series xix
    The Cards. xx
Introduction xxi
    Raising Our Energy xxii
    God and the Universe as Terms. xxiii
    The Layout of the Book and How to Use It xxv
    The Rose Path Meditations xxvi
    Guidance from Spirit xxvi
Chapter 1: The WOW Factor: Energy Mastery 1
    Driving through a Storm 2
    Blueprint to Mastering Energy. 2

    Mastering Your Mind: Receiving 3
    Storing, Plugging, Moving, and Defining Energy..... 5
    Rolling Sadness into Joy......................... 7
    Contracting Energy 8
    Moving energy 8
    Defining energy 9
    The "WOW" Factor............................ 10

Chapter 2: We Are WOW: Energy of Unity 13
    Alone Is Not the Same as Lonely 14
    Unity... 16
    The Energy Dance 18
    One Part of the Whole 21
    We versus I 22
    The Glow Stick............................... 24
    Sharing the Energy............................ 25

Chapter 3: Pow! To WOW: Energy of Power 29
    The Shopping Cart............................ 30
    Energy of Power 30
    Power and Lightness........................... 31
    Adding Lightness of Thought and Word 33
    The Power of No In and Out................... 36

Chapter 4: Vow to WOW: Energy of God Principle..... 41
    The Chalice 42
    The God Principle 43

Deep Dive into a Bubble 43
The I Am 46
I Am That. 47
How to Embody Source Energy. 49
God Is in All Things 50
Synchronicities 52
The Conditions: Experiment, Bus Stop, and
    Time Machines 53
The Inner Alchemist. 54

Chapter 5: How to WOW: Energy of Manifestation 57
The Shoelace 58
Manifestation 58
Space: The Final Frontier. 58
No Real Understanding 61
Dream: Magic. 64
No Need to Need 67
Spreading Peace 69

Chapter 6: Here and WOW: Energy of Transmuting. . . . 71
Teaching and Flowers 72
Higher and Lower Frequencies 72
Pet Peeves and Unity 73
The Wave Action: Anger, Fear, and Peace 76
Peace and Black Lives Matter 78
Clouds. 80

Letting Go of Dreams........................ 84

Chapter 7: Now to WOW: Purity of Energy........... 87

   Portals...................................... 88

   Pure Energy 88

   Energy and Understanding 92

   Energy and Food 99

   Language as Energy 101

   Fire Works 104

   What If It Is All Just a DANCE 105

Chapter 8: Allow WOW: Energy of Joyfinity 109

   A Pivotal Joy Experience 110

   Joyfinity: Acceptance, Gratitude, and Celebration . 111

   Laughing the Chakras 113

   Jellyfish Breathing........................... 115

   The Roll of Enlivening....................... 117

   The Energy of Joyfinity 119

Chapter 9: The WOW: of Sacred Technologies 121

   Chapter 1 Sacred Technologies: The WOW of
         Energy Mastery 122

   Chapter 2 Sacred Technologies: The WOW
         Energy of Unity 125

   Chapter 3 Sacred Technologies: The WOW
         Energy of Power....................... 126

- Chapter 4 Sacred Technologies: The WOW Energy of God Principle. 127
- Chapter 5 How to WOW: Energy of Manifestation 129
- Chapter 6 Here and WOW: Energy of Transmuting. 130
- Chapter 7 Now to WOW: Purity of Energy. 131
- Chapter 8 Allow WOW: Energy of Joyfinity 134

Appendix. 137
- Morning Prayer 137

The Pivotal Joy Experience. 139

Rikka Zimmerman's Six Principles. 141

The Rules of Energy. 143

Resources 145
- Online Resources 145
- Books. 145

Spiritual Practitioners 147

About Tricia Jeane Croyle. 149

Acknowledgments

I would like to thank my husband, John, of fifty-plus years, for his support in allowing me to take the time I need to write. And most of all for allowing me to grow and change as I learned to be myself.

I thank Rikka Zimmerman for giving me the opportunity to share my true nature on a larger stage.

I thank my fellow Life Transformed coaches for encouraging me to put myself out there.

I thank Leslie Sandra Black for being a true friend, and for keeping me going when I get stuck.

I would like to thank my editor Nina Shoroplova for turning my ramblings into an understandable reality.

I would like to thank all my coaches, guides, and animal friends that constantly remind me to stay on my path. And for getting in my face or tripping me when I don't.

Preface

From Eeyore to the Cheshire Cat

In 2014, I suffered a great deal of loss in a short period of time. I lost my mom, two horses, three dogs, and three cats. I had been taking care of my mother for three years. I had lost the rest of my family before that—John's mom (John is my husband), my brother, and my dad. My mother-in-law had lived with us for four years.

By the time I lost *my* mom, I needed to get away, and I was ready to travel. I felt a kind of freedom. I had a lot of suppressed grief. I went about my life thinking I was happy. After all, I was generally a happy person. But somehow my spark was gone, and I didn't even know it. I had pasted *happy* onto *sad*.

I attended a conference in 2015 where the people called me "Eeyore" (the sad donkey character from the Winnie the Pooh books). I spent a year trying to rekindle my sparkle. Sadness was leaking out of me, like a faucet that just wouldn't stop dripping. That year I discovered that it was necessary to allow myself to feel the grief and sadness so as to get through to the other side, which is Joy. It wasn't until later that I learned that life isn't something that happens *to* us; it is something that happens *for* us.

Then I had a pivotal experience. I call it the Pivotal Joy Experience. I describe this experience In the resources section at the back of the book. Suffice it to say that I would never be the same after that.

The Smile of the Cheshire Cat

My Pivotal Joy Experience gave birth to my Cheshire Cat smile. It seemed like I became just a smile, and nothing else. When I approached people, they saw the smile.

I was attending an architecture conference, speaking to a log home vendor about logs for a possible architecture project in Northern California when he said to me, "I just have to tell you, you have the most beautiful smile."

Then the following year at another conference, I walked into an evening buffet and drinks, a social hour. I sat down at a table and began a conversation with a young man. "Hi. How are you? Why are you here?"

It was that kind of chitchat conversation that occurs when people first meet.

After a few minutes, the young man said, "Wow! How can I be you? I want to be you. I want your life."

Fast forward to the evening of another architecture conference when I was sitting near the vendors. I had been researching a project I was working on in Maine—a passive, zero-energy house I was designing for a friend. I overheard a conversation a little way up the aisle from where I was sitting. It went like this: "You need to meet this woman. She is the most amazing woman. You just got to meet her."

The conversation went on.

I thought, *Boy, I need to meet this person they are discussing.* The one man saw me sitting there and motioned me over. He wanted to introduce me to the person he was talking to. And then it occurred to me. They were talking about me! OMG! They were talking about me. I walked over to meet his friend and then just walked away and shook my head. I wondered when I went from being Eeyore to having the smile of the Cheshire Cat, becoming a woman with a beautiful smile and someone somebody else wanted to be or to meet.

After the Joy Experience, I ran around telling people what I had experienced. I told them that I couldn't contain the Joy I was feeling. They told me not to contain it and to share it. And that is what I am doing. It is because of the grief and the subsequent Joy Experience that I am able to share. It has led to the creation of five books, four sets of meditation cards, and numerous classes. It has also led to the creation of an energetic system that I call "Joyfinity."

 Life isn't something that happens to us; it is something that happens for us.

The Joy Project

This is the fifth book in a project I call, The Joy Project. The Joy Project includes the Joy Series of four titles.

The Joy Series

From Heartache to Joy: One Woman's Journey Home

In the first book, *From Heartache to Joy: One Woman's Journey Home*, I explore my journey in discovering who I am and how I have allowed myself to come out into the world as an authentic being. I share my Morning Prayer and the exercises that developed out of that practice. I called these energies (sometimes referred to as *feelings*) as *aspects of God*, or of the Source of the Universe. Each aspect as I explored it became a pathway to explore myself and the energy that surrounded me as I explored it.

My first book identifies fifteen aspects of God Source, all of which, like spokes on a wheel, afford a path inward to the center of our being. Each aspect comprises a chapter.

Beyond Joy: A Journey into Freedom, Wisdom, Power, and Wellbeing

As I began to play with and explore the energies more and more, new aspects emerged, and I wrote the second book, *Beyond Joy: A Journey into Freedom, Wisdom, Power, and Wellbeing.* This book is a continuation of the exploration of the aspects of our God Source, with the addition of another twelve aspects, ranging from *Breath* to *Wonder*. In this book, I added to the aspects, the conditions that surround us, and the tools that we use. This second book in the series is much more of a *how-to* book, because it became apparent that people wanted to know how I had gone beyond the transformation of my sadness and grief into a Joyful being. I had gone beyond playing in the energy of Joy to the point where I could weave and dance with that energy.

From Heartache to Joy: A Companion Playbook

I wrote *From Heartache to Joy: A Companion Playbook* to accompany the first book. It offers more exercises than the first book and expands on them. It is full of exercises, puzzles, and quizzes, and is designed to be a workbook. I call it a playbook because I don't believe we can *work* our way to Joy; we can only play our way there. It is an oversized book for journaling.

Absolute Joy: A Journey Beyond Time to Nowhere

No longer were people calling me the *Cheshire Cat* instead of *Eeyore*. By now they were calling me the *Joy Magnet, Energy Dancer, Energy Weaver*, and most recently, *Dream Weaver of Worlds*. This ability to dance and weave pure energies is the result of experiencing absolute energy, *Absolute Joy*.

This book is about continuing to explore my path of *Absolute Joy*. It is also a journey of divine right timing to nowhere and to nothing.

In this third book in the Joy Series, *Absolute Joy*, I came to each of these pathways or aspects through direct experience by extensive practice of what I call the Morning Prayer, as well as through the exercises I shared previously. Most of the techniques are my own exercises, which came to me during meditations.

The Energy Series

Joyfinity is the first book in this new series, which I call the Energy Series.

Joyfinity: the WOW of energy mastery

In this first book in the Energy Series, I switch gears away from utilizing Joy as the main feeling aspect as the gateway into ourselves and I focus on pure energy states directly. I use the Sacred Technologies as the physical and mental activities that allow us to transform our thinking, beliefs, and bodies into higher energy states. Being in a higher energy state, we can direct our lives more efficiently without wasting energy, squandering our time, or getting stuck in the conditions that surround us. Higher levels of flowing energy allow us to blast through our current stagnated states to live our lives in freedom, flow, and fun.

The Cards

I created *The Morning Prayer Cards* and *The Rose Path Meditation Cards* to supplement the first three books. They can be found on my website, www.triciajeanecroyle.com. *The Morning Prayer Cards* accompany the first book. There are twenty-eight cards, each with an animal to represent the twenty-eight aspects of Source energy. *The Rose Path Meditation Cards* (seventy-eight cards in the deck) accompany both the first two books.

The third set is *The Rose Path Meditation Cards for Absolute Joy.* These cards accompany *Absolute Joy* with their truisms. Look for the *Joyfinity Cards* that accompany this book to come out soon. They will be available on my website, www. triciajeanecroyle.com.

Introduction

Introducing the Joyfinity System®

 Love matters before right or wrong.

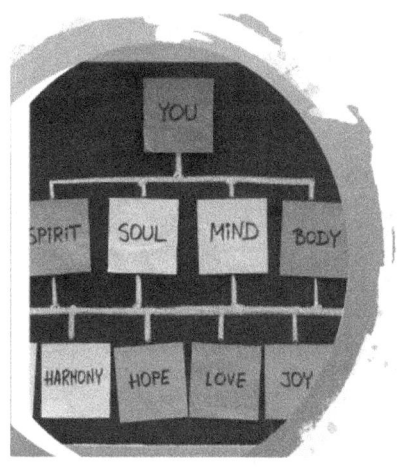

Align your body, mind, and spirit through acceptance, gratitude, and celebration.

Joyfinity is a term I use to describe a system to bring the body, mind, and spirit into alignment. This alignment allows us to gracefully experience the expansion of our higher frequencies and to utilize the focusing and grounding of our lower emotions to navigate life's challenges with fun and Joy. The alignment occurs with acceptance, gratitude, and celebration.

The *Joyfinity* System allows us to align the energies of our body, mind, and spirit with the energies of both heaven and earth, utilizing the rules of energy. This alignment allows us to run on all cylinders in our lives. We are always aligning the energies of source with ourselves. But often we are not doing it consciously. When we consciously realize we are truly aligning ourselves with our source, then we can emerge as who we really are—an evolving being of light with true freedom, true power, true abundance, and true Joy.

Raising Our Energy

How do we build or increase our energy? We align ourselves with the rules of energy. Like shamans and monks, we let go of self-importance, limiting beliefs, and judgements. Unlike monks, we live in a world of experiences and we allow these experiences to happen. We let go of the judgements we have about the experiences. Then we experience anew, and we allow. And then we let go of the judgement about each new experience. We repeat until we stand with Source at our backs in awe and wonder at all our experiences. Wonder dissolves the judgement. As do the transformative heart energies of unconditional Love and Joy.

I use the term *energy* in the names for each of the chapters because each is about the energy of the thoughts, words, and actions that we take. It is about the harmonization and elevation of these energies through our body and mind, and ultimately aligning these energies with our spirit.

God and the Universe as Terms

When I use the word *God* to describe the intelligent and conscious force of the Universe, I am not speaking about a deified God. I do not have a picture of God in my mind as if He were a deity or even masculine. I intend only to refer to the Source of us all. I sometimes use the term *Source of the Universe*, or the *Force*. Recently I began using the *Force* to see if the term worked better. It didn't. I find it easiest to use the word *God*. If this term disturbs you, please substitute *Source* or any other word you feel is appropriate. Using the word *God* works well when I talk about many of the aspects, because they are the feelings. Using *Universe* works better when I talk about the conditions; and *Force* works when I describe the energy. And yet, these terms are interchangeable.

When I think of the mind, the intelligence, or the truth, it just seems easier to speak about *God*. Previously when I had this conversation in my classes or books, I seemed to apologize for using the term *God*. I was careful because I didn't want to offend or turn off people who would otherwise be interested in what I was saying. But I no longer feel the need to apologize. I can't worry about sending people away. If I speak my own truth, others will choose to hear me or not.

At book fairs, I watch as people pick up my books and begin to read. They are trying to understand where I am coming from with my spirituality. They want to know if I am proselytizing Christianity. I've heard people say they are *not that spiritual*, especially when they begin to read my books. People are very sensitive to the language around the use of the terms *God* and *Universe*. I try to respect that sensitivity.

For instance, I call my morning practice, "my morning prayer." While my practice contains journeys, visualizations, breathing practices, and mental exercises, I still start with what I call a prayer. I start with gratitude and my own version of St. Francis of Assisi's prayer. That is why I call it my *Morning Prayer*. Then I have a ritual practice. The whole thing might last two hours or twenty minutes. I do this every morning as the sun is rising. But it really begins even before that, when I am waking up, wiggling my toes and hands to get them moving, and asking *What wondrous magical thing will happen today?*.

I continue with gratitude as I shower and brush my teeth, grateful for the warm water and my dry fluffy towel. And the wonderful toothpaste and the pink toothbrush my husband recently brought me from his latest trip to the dentist.

So even before I go downstairs to get a cup of gratitude-infused coffee, I am ready to give thanks for the coming day in my *Morning Prayer*.

Who am I praying to? God or the Universe? Yes. It is a yes to all and the only one. I like to call him God. It offends some that I don't say her. That I don't say *I call her God*. But that too seems exclusive. To call God *it* seems to offend me. So I say *He*.

There is plenty of rationale on both sides of the coin for referring to God as He or as She. Masculine energy is manifesting and expansive and active. Feminine energy is receptive and contractive. But then why is it so easy for women to walk a spiritual path? Because they are more in touch with their emotions. They are more easily able to receive and to allow. They are also more afraid to step into the expansion.

Both sides of the coin are needed. Expansion requires contraction whereas contraction makes you ready for expansion.

Some would call contraction *grounding*. Grounding focuses the energy. Consciousness expands the energy. Both are needed, like the jellyfish contracting to propel itself forward. There is a moment of suspension when it and we are neither expanding nor contracting. We just are. We pause. We pause in the heart of God or in the void or the gap.

The Layout of the Book and How to Use It

Unlike my other books, this one is less about thinking and more about taking action to align and integrate the energy of the body with the energy of the higher mind. First, we experience the energy. We do this in the body. Some would call this *embodiment*. Then we bring the thinking mind along. This book offers tools and techniques for integrating all energies. Some of the techniques in the final chapter provide more *how-to* detail than earlier chapters. The stories and examples are more about *what to do* than *why you are doing it* or *how you are doing it*. So the stories and examples are about the exercises and the experience of the exercises themselves.

How I come to these techniques is through visions and meditations. Then I try them and they work. I include the visions and meditations in italics so you can differentiate them from your reading and thinking mind. I continue to call the techniques *Sacred Technologies* because they are both sacred and physical technologies that bring about a spiritual alignment in the physicality of your being.

As with my other books, you may open this one anywhere and begin. You need not feel obligated to start at the beginning and work your way through. The ideas are circular in nature. All chapters are like spokes on a wheel and will lead you home to yourself. Experience what you want and for as long as you want and in any order you want. If you don't like one technique, move on to the next. You are not the same person this week as you were last week. Try something again that you tried before. It just might work differently this time. If you get in a rut with the same old exercise, try a new one. It matters more how you feel about what you are doing than about what you are doing. Energy is enlivened by our feelings. If you do the techniques with an expectation that they will be fun and will create a change, then they will. Expectation influences outcome.

The Rose Path Meditations

Throughout the book you will find sayings or quotes marked with a rose. These are meant to give you pause so you can think about them throughout your day. They are marked with a rose because that is the way I thank my guides for their help—I give each one a rose. I also give roses to my animal guides. It is simply the way I say, *Thank you.*

Some time ago, my guides started giving me roses in return—they saw fit to scatter roses on my path. So that is the way I find my path. I look for and smell the roses. And I give these roses to you. Each petal is meant to give you pause. To stop and smell. Sometimes, it is readily apparent why it is there. And sometimes, you will have to think about it. They are rather like koans or truisms. You are meant to meditate upon them.

Guidance from Spirit

I regularly check in with my Spirit Guides and the Universe for direction. This book shares some of the information I receive about the nature of mastering our energy and lives. I enjoy interacting with people who are "drawn to the light" and are committed to a life-purpose of personal growth and spiritual evolvement. If you would like to work with me, check my website at the end of the book.

This book is not meant to help everyone. I hope that this book will help those who are curious, willing, and committed to pursuing a path to energy mastery. My experience in this life work has shown me that as we commit to the process of elevating our vibration, our lives are transformed in positive ways.

My talent is to help people find their Joy and to raise, define, and refine their life's energy frequencies so that they may consciously cocreate their innermost dreams. Success is attained by holding fast to our conscious attention on our goals and by taking small, easy steps each day.

I lead by example, by successfully manifesting my own goals and dreams. I share my journey by bringing love and play to those around me through the Joy of living with ease and power.

Oh, yes, and every morning I take time to listen. I listen to the Universe.

Enjoy your journey as I enjoy mine and also enjoy sharing it here with you.

Authentically yours,
Tricia Jeane Croyle, AIA, BA, BED, MOB, ALTC

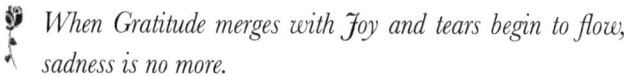 *When Gratitude merges with Joy and tears begin to flow, sadness is no more.*

CHAPTER 1

The WOW Factor: Energy Mastery

 The external world creates your life until it doesn't.

Energy Mastery

- Live by the rules of energy.
- Save your energy.
- Learn to define energy.
- Increase your energy.
- Play with energy.

Driving through a Storm

It was a four-hour drive to my mom's house through Wisconsin winters that can go really bad. Often there was a driving thunderstorm. I drove to Mom's house every week for three years. She was ninety-three at the end and needed my help to remain living in her assisted-living duplex. I would go down on a Wednesday and return on a Saturday. During bad weather, I would call on my guides, Gabriel and Garland, to help me out with the weather. I would ask, *Would you please stop the rain or snow for just a little while until I get past the traffic in Madison?* I want to arrive at my mother's house without an accident. And then in the next few minutes the snow or rain would stop or lessen, so that I could get to where I was going. As soon as the bad weather stopped, I would say *thank you*. And once I got through Madison, the blinding storm would start again.

I was grateful for what my guides had done for me. I was also in awe. We can feel gratitude. But when we add wonder and expectation, the magic happens. Our expectation focuses our intent, and the gratitude catalyzes the energy of our intent into motion. Is it magic? No, it is a kind of control over our emotions that I would call *energy mastery*. It's the transmuting of the fear energy toward bad weather and the anxiety energy of what might happen into the expectation energy of good weather so that by the time we ask for it, it is *already done*.

Blueprint to Mastering Energy

When you master your energy, you master your life. Your life becomes a WOW instead of a how—*How can I possibly do this? WOW, I can really do this!* All things are made of energy. This book is a blueprint for energy mastery. At least it is a beginning to energy mastery. In truth, we spend our lives learning to master our energy. Where do we start? First, we have to remove the blocks to accessing our energy. Then we need to plug the holes that are left when the blocks are gone. Then we need to store the energy. Then we need to get the energy moving! Then we can increase our energy. Then we can start to define and refine our energy. Then we can play and dance in that energy. There is an order to this. We can't let anything in if we first don't remove what's blocking it from coming in. For most of us, this starts with our minds.

Mastering Your Mind: Receiving

Receiving is an art form. Many healers are empaths, and they can easily take on the emotions of others. This is what makes them good healers. Empaths sometimes believe that the emotions of others are their own. For instance, I thought I was feeling the frustration of taking care of my mother when I was actually feeling her frustration of being in pain at the age of ninety-three. It was her frustration I was feeling and not mine in taking care of her. It's easy to confuse the feelings of another with your own, especially for empaths. We need to be aware of what another person is feeling. But we don't have to take it on, and we don't want to confuse ourselves into thinking it is our own.

One way to know the difference is to ask the question, *Is this a feeling that I choose to feel?* If not, then it is probably a feeling belonging to someone else. If the answer is yes. Then enjoy it or let it go.

To be on the *new earth* we must be in it from a different place. We have to move into this other place. How? We embody our soul's vibration. When working with another as a lightworker, we hold the space for them to experience the soul, the God Principle. This is what healers do. They first raise the energy of the person and then they bring their client's mind along.

We need to stay open in order to receive. To do this, say, *I now choose to receive ... Love.* We create the *new world* in the quantum world, not in the thinking world. When we consciously breathe, we integrate the light of that world into the body.

Then we let the higher energy state hold us. We don't hold the energy state. It's too much work to hold the space. Instead, let the space hold you. This allowing is practicing the art of receiving. Trying to hold on to something or to control another person contracts your energy and stops it from flowing.

When you practice the art of receiving into your heart and brain, it allows you to be in divine right timing and the flow. We each do our own upgrade. We upgrade by receiving more and higher energies. When we allow more receiving, we allow more energy.

Sacred Technology for Increasing Receiving

- **Choose receiving.** Say, *I now choose to receive ...* Love (or health or wealth). Say whatever you would like to receive. Say it three times. You could also say, *I choose to receive receiving.*
- **Feel receiving.** Breathe in slowly and out slowly as you count to seven. Do this seven times. Feel the energy of

receiving as you inhale; feel the letting go as you exhale and create more room for more receiving.

Storing, Plugging, Moving, and Defining Energy

Storing and Saving Energy

Once we remove the blocks and are able to receive, then we need to store and conserve our energy. Embodying the energy is one way to do this. One of my favorite ways to embody energy is to visualize energy when I swim laps at a local pool. Any repetitive exercise done while visualizing or repeating a mantra works. You will find more examples later. Here I offer you this: swimming your breaststroke of energy. You can embody energy by saying a mantra while you exercise. I like to say, *You are love. You are light. You are infinite.* When I am exercising, I do this with every step I take or with every stroke I swim. This has the effect of embodying the energy of the mantra.

Sacred Technologies: Swim your Energy

- **Do the breaststroke with your energy.** See it move as you pull your arms down to your side, when the tips of your fingers meet. Roll the backs of your hands together in a kind of reverse praying action. Then raise them up over your head and turn them out. See your energy moving as you do this. Add your breath to the exercise. Breathe in as you pull your arms down and exhale out as you push the energy up and out through your crown chakra. You can make this as big as you like, dropping the energy way below your feet and way above your head. Do at least forty *energy breaststrokes.* This will get the channeled energy moving smoothly. Your energy is already doing this, and you are just consciously participating in moving it along. Adding this movement with your conscious breathing will assist you in embodying source energy.

Swim the Breaststroke and Add Your Conscious Energy

- **Breaststroke in the pool.** Swim the breaststroke with your conscious breathing and mantra energy when you are in the water. This will get the energy moving smoothly along the core of your being. Adding your conscious breathing with this movement will assist you in embodying source energy. Adding a mantra will bring your mind along into the exercise. Add the mantra: *I am open to receiving energy.* Time this mantra with the movements of your breaststroke.

Plugging Holes

We don't want to leak our energy. Emotions not only block energy from coming in—they also create holes where energy can leak out. Our energy is lower when we feel anger, hate, or envy than when we love. Our energy leaks because we are attaching it to something outside us. We might be giving our energy to that which is outside us, like another person we envy or a situation we dislike. There might be something we can't let go of, like when somebody tries to harm us. We need to plug those holes. We need to bring our focus and our energy back into ourselves. The following exercises can be used to return our energy and plug the holes.

Sacred Technology: Return Your Energy

- **Quit leaking energy.** Pull your energy back to yourself consciously. Say, *I now bring all my energy back to me, clean, clear, and abundant.* Say this three times.

Rolling Sadness into Joy.

When you physically roll and contract your body you are moving energy. Then you shift to just contracting and rolling the energy without the physical contraction. And then you graduate to just noticing yourself rolling the energy. The movement itself plugs the holes. This activity is also good for moving, defining, and increasing energy. Rolling is a great exercise for all aspects of flowing energy.

In this practice, I roll sadness from the second chakra up into the heart and then I drop it down. This mixes happiness into sadness. Then I roll it up into the throat, which is closer to Joy, and then I drop it down and then I roll it up into the third eye and drop it down. Then it is bliss energy mixing with the sadness and Joy energy. Then I roll it up into the crown. I call the crown the *I-don't-know* energy. So I would be mixing *I-don't-know* energy with the energy below.

Sacred Technology: Roll Sadness into Joy

- **Rolling sadness into Joy.** Think of something sad. Feel where the sadness is located in your body. Is there a contraction or burning somewhere? Contract physically or lift the sadness up to your heart chakra. Let it drop back down. Roll it up to your throat. How does it feel there? Let it go back down. Roll it up to your third eye. How does it feel there? Let it fall back down. Roll it up to your crown chakra. How does it feel there? Let it go back down.

- **Reverse direction.** You can also flow the energy in the other direction with a simple noticing. Notice your crown chakra and then notice your sacral chakra. Notice wherever you are holding sadness. Then allow the energy from your crown chakra to flow down into the sacral chakra. This is not a physical contraction of the body. It is simply the noticing of your energy. How does that feel? Repeat the noticing of the energy dropping down from the heart, throat, and third eye chakras.

Contracting Energy

Every time we expand our energy, we also need to let it contract. This keeps us in balance. What goes up, must come down What goes out, must come in. If we don't consciously contract our energy, our body will do it for us, by utilizing the lower energies of hate or greed. We can avoid this experience by choosing to ground ourselves. One way to do this is to consciously ground our energy.

Sacred Technology for Grounding: Tickle the Earth.

- **For grounding.** Feel into the earth with the energy of your feet. Tickle the center of the earth. Take a deep breath. Do this three times.

Moving energy

One of the rules of energy is that it has to move. We can't hold our energy in one place. It can't be contained or constrained.

Anything that moves your body, moves your energy. You can dance or go for a walk. The following techniques will also get your energy moving:

Sacred Technology for Moving Energy

- **Move energy in a triangle**. Open your palms and see the sun above your head, your mind in your right palm, and your spirit in your left palm. Circulate the energy around the triangle. See it as a white ball moving from apex to apex. And then see it as a continuously moving stream of light. Then change directions.
- **Slinky**: See your hands held out with a slinky in them. This is a kind of toy where you can raise your hands up and down one at a time and the slinky will fall to one side or the other. Now imagine that you have an energetic slinky the colors of the rainbow. Play with that rainbow raising one hand up and down and then the other so that the rainbow flows back and forth into the opposite hand. Inhale and exhale as you do this. Now feel the energy flowing up and down your body as you play with your slinky. Continue until you have the energy in your body moving.

Defining energy

Before we can really start to dance with energy, we need to know who or what we are dancing with. We need to define the energy with us. Is it Peace or Love or Joy? These are all distinct energies. Doing the Morning Prayer and asking to be shown the energies is a good way to learn to define them (see the Morning Prayer in the Appendix). We can also do some exercises with the senses.

Sacred Technologies: Identifying Energy Using the Senses

- **Define peace.** Is it hot or cold? or neutral? Is it fast moving or slow moving or barely moving at all? What color is it? Try it on like a cloak. And then take it off. Put on another feeling energy like Joy. What color is it? How does it differ from peace?
- **Food energy.** Now try something like lemon zest. Feel, smell and taste lemon zest. What kind of energy is it? When you begin to salivate, you know that you are embodying the energy. This is proof that your body is reacting to your thoughts and your energy.
- **Temperature and directions.** Feel yourself as hot and cold. Then feel all four energies of wind, earth, water, and sun. Face all four directions, north, south, east and west. What color is each? Is it hot or cold, warm or dry? Can you differentiate between east and west energy? North and south energy?

Energy truly has no constraints. It only has properties. When it has certain properties, we decide to call it Peace or Joy. Practice defining the energy around you. Then let it go back into being just energy.

The "WOW" Factor

Being *just energy* is no small thing. In fact, it is more like Wow! This is why I have used the *WOW Factor* of energy in the name for each of the chapters. The *WOW of Unity* energy allows us to increase our energy by uniting with all things. The *WOW of Power* energy shows us how to increase the power of our energy while keeping it soft and easy. The *WOW of God Principle* energy shows us how to align with the natural laws: the laws of energy and the laws of the Universe. The *WOW of Manifestation* shows us how to utilize the mindset of allowing ourself to focus and create the life we want to live. The *WOW of Transmuting* energy explains the inner alchemy of negative energies into more positive energies to live a life filled with freedom and fun. The *WOW of Pure Energy* shows us how to define and refine the energies that surround us. And finally, the *WOW of Joyfinity* is the celebration of the experience when we take the pure Joy energy and ride it on into the infinite. The *WOW of Sacred Technologies* provides the tools to do this.

 We each do our own upgrade.

CHAPTER 2

We Are WOW: Energy of Unity

 Soften and allow the path.

Each energy is a path on the wheel. All lead to the center.
Peace, Joy, Wellness, Abundance are but a few. At the center is zero point. And all that is. Which spoke is yours?

Alone Is Not the Same as Lonely

Are you alone and feeling lonely? As I watch many people on television talk about being home and not able to go out to restaurants and work because of the Corona Virus, I hear them complain about being lonely. Especially the extroverts. I'm an introvert. But even I am beginning to want to go out to a restaurant. I love to go out to lunch. I am retired, so I don't have the pressure of having to go out.

Introversion and Extroversion

Even an introvert can be tired of being alone. Usually, I can go three days without seeing someone other than my husband. He, the extrovert, is suffering under these "stay at home" conditions. He often goes out and has several meetings a day with people. He even over schedules himself so that he goes from meeting to meeting without a break. Many are at the same time. So, he goes to one for half the time and the other for the second half.

What does this tell us? He hates being alone? Or as an extrovert he gains energy by being with people? He seems to only have energy for projects that involve people.

I remember my mom telling me that although she was alone for many years in her life. she was not lonely, even though I "abandoned" her (my words) when I lived overseas for two years. And then for another five years.

Now, she was an extrovert! Mother could talk to any stranger in a grocery line, and the people at the next table in a restaurant always chatted with her. So, she was not lonely. She said that she loved being alone with herself. She liked herself.

She didn't need the distractions of other people to keep her from her own thoughts. While there seems to be more pressure on the extrovert being alone, either because they are an extrovert or because they are in lockdown, I don't think that is necessarily the case. How we perceive the pressure of *being alone* or in *lockdown* is more telling.

An Opportunity

I also *like* being alone. I love my private time to meditate and think my thoughts. My days are filled with a myriad of projects that I can do or not do. I don't need the distractions of the world to keep me from myself or my thoughts. This time of self-isolation is an excellent opportunity for many people to get to know themselves better. Also, it is a time to get to know their families who are sequestered with them. And it has proved to be a time when people who are not sequestered with their families reach out and get closer.

I am also aware that the times I have felt the loneliest were when I was in large groups of people. At least this was true earlier in my life. I felt the loneliest when I was in the midst of a party. I now enjoy speaking one-on-one with people, even at a party. But not so much in a group. Having taught for twenty years, I am comfortable in front of a group. So, for me, the introvert, being with a group of people does not affect the level of my loneliness. So, what does instill a sense of loneliness?

I believe it has to do with the level of comfort we feel about being with ourselves. There are many people reaching out because they are stressed in this time of pandemic quarantine. Yes, many financial hardships are happening. And people are struggling because of a lack of food and low financial welfare.

It is up to those of us who are more fortunate to help those in need. But I am not writing about those stressors, the stressors of lack. I am writing about being alone and not being lonely. Take this alone time as a good opportunity to get to know yourself as well as your family. You have the time and you have the opportunity.

Sacred Technology: Being Happy with Being Alone

- Ask yourself, *What do I fear in being alone?*
- Ask yourself, *What is it that I don't want to know about myself?*
- Then forgive yourself for whatever it is. Say, *I forgive myself for …*
- Say, *I am okay with being alone.*
- Say, *I even like being alone.*
- Say, *I cherish this time that I have to be alone.*
- Ask, *Who am I?*

Unity

Unity is a state of mind. Oneness. It is about combining all parts into one. It is the absence of diversity and the uniformity of character. It is also the mathematical numeral 1. And a quantity regarded as *one*, according to any dictionary. I also think that unity is about the fact that we are never really alone because we are always in contact with the Universe. Unity happens when we give up living in a dualistic world and choose to step forward into a loving world where all decisions are made from Love and the expressions of Love like Peace and Joy.

Unity and Separation

The journey I took during this morning's practice was once again to my sacred garden, the stage. I have decided to share it because it is about the difference between Unity and separation or as I like to think of separation, duality.

Vision

I look out at the audience. I am smiling and very happy to be back here. And then I am a dragon. Dragon flames come out of my mouth.

"Did you see that?" I ask the audience. "Dragon is here."

And then Turtle shows up and a small Otter appears to my left. I thank all the animals that have begun showing up. I recognize that people are sharing their animal spirits with me. Or more accurately, the animals that are the people's guides are sharing themselves with me. Some people in the audience are aware of it, but most aren't. And then I say "Stop. You are all welcome."

Uma the beluga whale shows up. She rises up out of the water. Her name comes to me even though I know that there is no naming, and I should call her simply "Beluga Whale" in the shamanic tradition of calling in archetypes and not naming individuals. But I call her Uma anyway. I don't question names or naming. And I know she comes here for Nikole Kadel.

I ask, "What message do the animals have for me and does one of them want to speak?" They all speak at once and I can't separate everything out. So, I ask for one of them to answer my question: "What is the best thing for this group to hear today?"

> *Uma, the whale says, "Have fun." So, I say, "Okay. Let's have some fun!"*
>
> *The fun begins with my explaining to people about energies and the three categories that I put them in. Energy really has no definition or category. It is more like a fuzzy fog. We simply put the energies into categories so that we can play with them. There is really not an energy like "struggle" or "hate" or "fear." Although it seems like there is because we certainly feel those things.*

Nikole Kadel is an energy healer and light worker who leads people on trips to Tonga where she facilitates them in spiritual journeys swimming with the whales. She has a very calm, earth-centered energy. She has both whale and bear spirit guides.

The Energy Dance

The vision continues. I watch as I wave my hands in the air. My hands dance the explanations as my mouth speaks them.

> *"On the left there is struggle and on the right there seems to be peace. But really there is no peace on the right. There is only 'no struggle' on the right. Peace is in the middle."*
>
> *Then I show "anger and hate" on the left. On the right there seems to be Love. But no. There is only "no hate" and "no anger" on the right. In the middle there is Love. But wait. Love is at the top. Love is at the center of all energies. Love is the seed or the Source energy. When we go deeply enough into*

any energy, we find Love. Love contains all energies. It is at the center and the heart of all energies.

And then a shower drops down from the Source in the sky and all the rivulets or streams of water rain down on me and I am filled with all the energies of love. Each one falls into a category of energy. One is Joy and another is Peace and another is Harmony.

Feelings like hate, anger and fear are not aspects. They are just feelings. They don't really exist on their own. We see them and we pick them up. We can simply put them down. And pick up a feeling energy that feels better.

"Unity is at the source and I call that unity Love. There are many aspects of Love and I give these the names of feelings, such as Peace and Joy. And then there are conditions and I call these conditions Freedom and Power. And there is also the category of tools like the Breath and Laughter. I only categorize them so that I can play with them. They are really just energies, like fog. And with the dashboard of all energies in front of me, I simply pick one up and give it a name like Peace. I give it a color and a taste and a smell. So that I can experience the energy of it. I have to define it to experience it and I do. I define the energies and I put them in the categories so that we can understand them. But there is really no understanding. How about knowing? Yes, we can know them. But I believe we can know them best by playing with them and experiencing them. So, I do."

Vanilla Ice Cream

I decide to offer the audience a grand buffet of a seven-course meal with all its gourmet complexities. But no. I hesitate. I choose instead simplicity. Then, in my energy body, I stand in front of each member of the audience individually. And I offer them a spoonful of vanilla ice cream. I stop. I smell popcorn. Someone has thrown popcorn with melted butter into the energy mix. I laugh. Always someone tries to mix it up. And then there are Cheetos. My personal favorite junk food. "No" I say. "Stop. The flavor is God's energy. We are having vanilla ice cream."

They open their mouths as I open mine. I feel the cool ice cream melting as it slides down my throat. And the delicious smell of vanilla. So simple. "What does God taste?" I ask. And the "yum-mm" goes down throughout my body and all our bodies.

I wait, and then I bring back all my selves to me. Snap, snap, snap, like rubber bands. I pull in a few stragglers that haven't quite returned. And I take a deep breath.

The energy of Unity is the energy of God or Love, which is all energies. We separate the energies in order to experience them. When we experience them we become them. And then we reflect them back to Source. And Source gets to know the energies more clearly through our experiences.

Sacred Technology: Energy of Ice Cream

Ice cream energy. Eat ice cream or any other fun food with the intent of having fun. Eat it slowly with the intent of having pleasure. Allow it to melt and meld with your body. Ask God what the ice cream tastes like. How does it feel as it goes down? Listen to what Source has to tell you about this. Know that it nourishes your body at the same time that it is fun to eat.

One Part of the Whole

One part of the whole is a drop of water that resides in the ocean. A leaf on a tree amidst all the leaves of all the trees. A rock of the earth resting on a mountain. A spark of fire residing in a volcano which resides with the molten center of the earth. A breath of air which comes from all of space and returns to it.

One cell is a part of the whole. The cell resides with all of the cells of the body. One man a part of all of humanity. Humanity is one part of all of life and all that is. One planet is a part of all planets and one universe a part of all universes.

The drop of water has the backing of the power of the ocean. The leaf in the tree has the power and knowledge of all of the tree. And perhaps many trees. All that is contained in the mountain is contained in the rock. The rock is the hologram of the whole. One mountain contains all of the energy of all mountains. One spark contains all the energy of the volcano. The volcano contains all the energy of the molten center of the earth. All the memory. The memory of the beginning of the planet erupting out of the central sun. The memory contains the Truth of the law of the Universe.

One single breath of air can change the life force of the body. Our breath is closest to spirit. It is *inspiritus* and *inspiration*. One cell divides and reproduces itself in divine perfection.

Divine perfection is eternal reproduction and therefore eternal life. One man living a life of Love is in Divine Perfection and reproduces himself in the same way as the cell.

The energy of the one raises the energy of those around him. All are connected in the matrix of life and the grand scheme of the Universe. It has been said that *we are only as great as the least among us*. It is also true that we can be as great as the greatest amongst us and even greater. Jesus spoke similar words. A great individual raises the energy of those around him. The other has but to make a choice. The choice is to accept and choose gratitude for the greatness that we all already are.

I have often shared the metaphor of the one drop in the ocean. But here I have offered all the elements together, one part of the great vast planet and universe and cosmos. We are all made of those elements physically. The physical transformation into pure crystalline energy can occur with one thought, a very powerful thought. It can also come from many thoughts all headed in the same direction. One word. Or many songs sung in the praise and celebration of the eternal Love of God the Universe. *God the Man* sings this song to the Universe and *God the Universe* is silent, although those that also celebrate the Glory can be heard. There must be silence to hear them sing. I raise up my consciousness to sing Love. My song joins with the chorus of the heavens. We are one together.

We versus I

We is just an inclusion of the other. I think of Esther Hicks's use of the word *We* in her telling of what she knows. At first it seems a bit clumsy. But I understand that she was bringing in the truth from another side, from the other. Many say that it is from Abraham, another being. What her *We* refers to doesn't matter to me. What I do find significant is the use of the word *We*. It is often said that *where two or more are gathered* something powerful happens. That is true. But I am discussing our belief in separation or our trying to separate ourselves from the whole.

All our cells make up our body. The body represents the individual as a unity. All of the humans make up the body of humanity. We are like the cells. We are one humanity.

We seems to include all. But in fact, *I* is the only unity and inclusive factor. The unity of *I* is the most inclusive. It says that there doesn't need to be any gathering of individuals to make a *We*, whether it is one or two or the *We* of the Universe of God. There is only the "*I*" that exists everywhere with all points being the source point. *I am that.*

Open the Door Inward

The answer is not looking out. It is looking inside of us. Everything we need is inside of us. Every time you do this exercise, you will step forward and forward will be into yourself.

Sacred Technology: Unity

Open the door inward. Pull your awareness back against your spine. Look forward. See a door. Go toward the door and open it inward. Turn around facing back to yourself and see yourself. Turn around and look forward. Step back against your spine. See another door. Open the door inward. Turn around and see yourself standing there looking out. Turn forward and look out. See another door. Open it inward. Turn around and face yourself. Then turn forward and look out. See another door. Repeat ten times.

The Glow Stick

I am standing onstage in Ojai. I tell the audience to imagine they have a glow stick that runs from their crown chakra to their root chakra. It is glowing. Tiny gold tendrils run out of the ends of the glow stick. Tendrils also run out of all our chakras that surround the glow stick and connect with the universal matrix.

This is the way we are connected to all that is. We receive and send information, our thoughts, and our desires through these very fine golden lines. Try this as an exercise.

Joining Glow Sticks

I am experiencing a contraction in the first and second chakras. I roll the energy from the first chakra up and join it with the energy from my crown chakra. This is Christ Consciousness. The energies seem to meet at my heart and throat. At first, I contract it out of my body. The next time this happens, I let it fall back down and I see residue left over from the cleansing of the crown energy hitting the root energy. I repeat. Then the next time I realize that the energy around the root chakra is transformed and that there is no residue. Then I go back to the glow stick technique.

I tell the audience to allow the glow stick to glow and then all of our glow sticks are so bright that they begin to join and overlap. I tell the audience they must accept that we are united as one. If they don't, they don't have to join, but they must choose on their own. However, I know that the energy in the room is so high that most will not refuse. So, I continue.

I ask them to say "I accept. I accept the light of God. We are one because our lights are so bright and so expansive now that we have joined."

Of course, I know that we already are this way. But to accept out loud is to accept the will and power of being the children of God. We are all children of God.

When I see the light expand, it is so bright that all are truly one.

And so it is. And so it is. And so it is. Now and forever. My hands move only slightly in the energy of "so it is." It is like both hands are grasping a rope lightly with my fingers pulling the rope into my body. And then my hands move in a firm downward pounding of a staff on the words of "now and forever more."

Sharing the Energy

Later when I play with the up and down light of the glow stick, I bring the light up the stick and join it with the Christ consciousness of the crown chakra and send it out of my mouth down to the earth.

I find that I am up above the earth looking down. I send all the conditions of God, like Peace and Love and Joy, to all those on the earth who are willing to receive. And I find that I myself have received these energies also.

And the energies and I have grown because it is with the joining with others that we ourselves grow into the light. And we have done this. I repeat it many times. Sometimes sending it out of my mouth and sometimes out of my power chakra, the solar plexus.

> *I look down at the earth enmeshed as it is in a fine mist of Peace, Love, and Joy. I stand back and find that I am holding hands with millions of angles and we are surrounding the earth at the equator. We dance to the right and we dance to the left and then we lean back and then we lean forward. And we blow the energies of Peace Love and Joy down onto the earth. We do it several times. Our breath becomes a fine mist and falls on all who are on the earth. The energy level of the earth is raised. People look around and some say. "Oh, I feel more peaceful now."*

And so it is. And I also feel more peaceful now.

So, what is the WOW of Unity energy? It is about being alone and not feeling lonely. It is about never being separate because we are always in contact with God and our higher self. It is about feeling the Peace, Love, and Joy when we are connected. It is about knowing that we are one part of a whole with the power of the whole behind us. It is about the language of *we* trying to be inclusive while the *I* within already contains all that is. Unity is to be found as we look inside ourselves and then join with the other outside us. And then, with the joining, there is no *outside us*, only unity. The same can be said of our nation joining with other nations to find peace. True power resides in the unity of peace. I would call that a WOW!

> *The US is like a toddler learning to walk spiritually. We are working our way into peace and unity.*
>
> —Dr. Sue Morter

CHAPTER 3

Pow! To WOW:
Energy of Power

 We don't get what we want by fighting for it.

Power

The Shopping Cart

It is early spring, 2014, and I am pulling into a parking space at a grocery store in Rockford, Illinois. The last traces of slush and snow are disappearing into the drainage basins. I have escaped from my mom's house to do her grocery shopping. I need a break from taking care of her. I am frustrated about being told what, when, and how to do everything.

But I can't pull all the way into the parking space because a grocery cart is in the way. And I can't back out because a car is pulling out behind me. I am stuck!

So, I wait. Then I get fierce and wave my finger as if it is an invisible magic wand at the cart and I yell at it. *Move. Damn it!* It doesn't move. *Great,* I think. *My magic wand isn't working. OK then. Some person could move it for me.*

And right then a man walks by, grabs the offending cart, and moves it out of the way. I am dumbfounded.

I quickly thank the universe for answering my request and give a little chuckle.

We think the Universe should respond in a certain way. It always responds—but it responds in its own way. The Universe does have my back. My magic wand is working. The Universe always supports us.

Energy of Power

What is the energy of Power? It is an energy that resides within us. This energy is the most powerful when it is light and not forced. It is directed by our attention, focused by our intention, and held in place or sustained by our will.

Our level of energy fuels our Power. Our emotions fuel our energy. This is our intensity. God has already given us infinite Power. We only need to remember it. And we must not waste or dissipate it.

We conserve and increase our energy by not wasting it on negative feelings like hate and greed. We increase our energy by staying in the present moment and by adding higher energy emotions or feelings like Peace and Love to our Power. Our words and thoughts have Power and when spoken with the highest good in mind, they increase our power. Gossip and anger decrease our Power. While anger feels powerful because it is contracted, it is a destructive force. Anger not only wreaks havoc on those around us but it also wreaks havoc on the person expressing it.

Power and Lightness

I used to think of Power as something absolute like an atomic bomb and because it felt so heavy, I wished to lighten it with something light like a feather. I combined the two energies so that I would have a light way of powerfully interacting with the world.

This idea first came to me in a dream where I was screaming at one of my guides because I thought that he couldn't hear me. He just looked at me and said, *You know, there's nothing wrong with my ears. You don't have to scream. You could just whisper.* For me that was the beginning of playing with lightness and noticing.

Today when I thought of how I am a humble drop of water with all the power of the ocean behind me, I also combined power and lightness. But this image is more about smallness and greatness. The power of Gandalf saying, *You shall not pass* or the power that comes from an atomic bomb are supreme. But those supremely powerful energies feel too heavy to carry around. So, I ask myself, *How do I infuse lightness into the magnitude of power? Is there an answer that is hidden in the similarities of the metaphor for the drop of water being backed by the ocean?* The answer is Love. I can insert Love into Power and I have a very flexible, penetrating and emanating form of power. And I can carry that power around with me.

So, I try this. Which do I start with? Do I add Power to Love, or Love to Power? If I stand forth in Power, I add a little Love. If I stand forth in Love, I allow it to radiate with Power and thus I have combined them. It depends on where you stand when you ask the question. It makes no difference how you get there. It only matters that you get there. I think that I like starting with Love and adding Power to it. I am reminded that pure Love is a force of its own and needs no added Power. So, I think that this is the answer. If I find myself standing in too much power, I might need to soften it just a bit with Love. If I find myself in pure Love, I need nothing else. There is nothing more powerful than pure Love.

Sacred Technology: Infuse Love into Power

Cherish and power. See yourself standing on the top of a mountain at the top of the world. You look down and admire all that you have created. You are, after all, on the top of your world. Soften this feeling with Love and cherish all that you see below you. Feel the softness that Love brings without any relinquishing of power.

 Give Love a path so that it doesn't have to rise up in revolt.

Adding Lightness of Thought and Word

Meditation on the Rose Path Meditation Cards

I sit in front of an audience and I am explaining the Rose Path Meditation Cards. How they came into being. "They are like Koans," I tell the audience.

But no, they are more like guideposts for your path. Koans seem to have a twist in them that tends to twist the mind. These Rose Path Meditation Cards function more like directional guideposts. I think of the wooden signs that people put on arrow-shaped pieces of wood stacked up on posts with their names and the names of their cabins. I live in Northern Wisconsin, where people put small signs directing others to their homes and cabins on the lake or in the woods. Sometimes when you pass a gravel road, you will see ten of these signs stacked up on one post. They point the way to several people's homes. They resemble the red and white lake markers that point the direction away from danger in the water to a safe path of travel.

I think that my rose path sayings are like that too. They point the direction away from danger and home to ourselves. But I have not called them signs. I call them Rose Path Meditations. I call them that because when I first started calling in the animals and giving them names or hearing what their names were …

> *And here they are now. I am surrounded by hundreds and now thousands of animals and human guides. I started with animal guides instead of human guides. I feel closer to them. Jesus is also in my heart. I see him there. He stands with a lion on one side and a lamb on the other. So, I still am connected to the animals. Did I give them names or did I hear their names? It makes no difference.*

The Power occurs when we say the name, whether it is *Whale* in the shamanic tradition or *Uva* by name. They appear. The Power is in stating the name *Uva* or *Whale*. When you say it, they appear. The spoken word has Power. This is why I have you repeat things out loud. The energy of the mind also has Power.

> *Or is it really the energy of the inner spirit directing the energy of my focus? This is not the energy of the mental mind.*

The spoken word comes from the mental mind and the directed energy from the inner spirit. Both word and energy have power and are joined together.

So. Why do I call them *Rose Path Meditation Cards*? I call them that because of my experiences with my guides. They are here. And they think it is better to show you than to explain it to you. So.

> *"Okay, what do you have to say?" I ask.*

"We just said it. It is better to show than to tell."

"Thank you for that." I reply. And in gratitude, I give them each a rose. There are thousands of them, and I give them a thousand roses. All the roses get thrown up into the heavens and they rain back down like rose petals on a path. My path. I love roses and I get to follow a rose-petal-strewn path. I smell them and I see that they turn to the right and I turn to the right.

The sayings are meditations that can focus your path in a certain direction. As I wrote, I would all of a sudden stop and say, *Hmm. That's interesting. I should repeat that.* And then I did and the Rose Path Meditations were created.

Power also comes when thousands of guides surround us. As we call out their names, we notice them, and their power joins ours. Their energy has combined with ours.

Power: Joining Forces.

A tornado swirls in front of me. The water rises up and I hold it back like Moses parting the waters. It is a 200 foot high ocean wave holding its curl in space and time. The earth erupts with a spewing volcano. And I stand in the middle, choosing to direct or choosing to not direct this confluence of powerful energy.

Then I step back and breathe. "Peace," I say. And I feel the gentle mist of rain. A breeze moves across my face and moves my hair into my eyes. I pick up the moist wet earth for planting a bulb. The warm sun shines down upon my face. And I exhale.

What a contrast these two energies are. The one that I will call Peace, and the other that I name Power. *What would happen, I wonder, if I placed the energy of Power inside the energy of Peace?* I move my fingers slightly in all four directions inviting the energies of earth, wind, fire, and water into the subtle energy of Peace, which also has those energies. The energy of Power recognizes the energy of Peace in the realm of wind and they become one. So, with the tiny flick of my finger the gentle breeze could have behind it the torrent of a tornado, if I so chose to release that energy.

Trying to control that amount of energy would require an equal and opposite amount of energy. But by joining it with the gentle energy of Peace, I can simply direct it with a subtle nudge of my fingers. It becomes easy. The same is true for the other elements—fire, earth, and water.

Remember: a whisper speaks much louder than a scream. A whisper can contain the power of a tornado and we have added the energy of sound!

The Power of No In and Out

There is no difference between In and out. Or more specifically what is inside us and what is outside us. There is only our perception of it. We think of Power as being held in or contracted until it bursts forth in a kind of explosion. That is the way power works in a bomb or in propulsion. But that isn't true Power. True Power comes from the *focus* of an ever so slight *motion*. The contraction power is replaced by the focus power. Focus is a kind of contraction. So instead of contracting before the release, we can focus on the ever so slight movement that is the motion of the release. Focus is a narrowing down of our intent and attention.

Rolling Sadness into Joy without Contracting

Performing the exercise of rolling sadness into Joy without contracting actually increases the power of the energy. When I perform the exercise that I call "rolling sadness into Joy," I first contract my physical body by rolling the contraction from my lower belly up through my heart area. Then I replace the physical roll with an energetic one and roll it all the way out my crown. I see myself roll up through my body with a rolling contraction. I also see myself just making a similar slight rolling motion with my hand in unison with the contraction. I am ever so slightly rolling my fingers upward in a similar but ever so tiny movement.

The movement with my fingers is almost imperceptible. Why am I doing this? Because It is easy. And because Power comes from easy and not from a contracted constraint. So, I ask myself, could I simply move my fingers ever so slightly and accomplish the same contraction energy as I had with my belly doing the contracting? Yes, I can. Why do it this way? Because it is sustainable, and it is easy. I like easy. It is also more powerful.

Sacred Technology: Increased Lightness Using Your Fingers

Move energy with your fingers. Roll sadness into joy by physically contracting your body and rolling the contraction upward. Then let it drop back down. Do this three times. Then Roll the energy of sadness without the contraction from a lower chakra where you have stored it up into a higher chakra such as your heart or third eye chakra. Roll your sadness up into joy. And then let it drop back down bringing the Joy down into where the sadness was held. Do this three times. Then do it with the simple motion of your fingers. Do it outside yourself with your fingers and notice the energy flow. See how small and light you can make the movement.

Expand In and Out

There is another exercise that also facilitates the raising of the frequency of your Power. I have spoken many times about "contracting in and expanding out" with our energy. We often raise our hands up to receive the joyous energy that drops down on us from the Heavens. We take that energy in. We also see ourselves dropping into the center of our beings to discover what is there. But what if there is no outside? And there is no inside?

What if I can move my finger and move the energy just an inch from *out there* to *over there*? What if my inside is really *out there* and what if *out there* is really *in here*? And what if there is no *out there* and *in here*? Then what? I can easily play *out there* and know that it is *in here*. And I can rain down the Joy of God knowing that it is coming from *inside* and going to *inside* and all of it is really *out there* and *in here* at the same time. Where does that leave me?

There is no difference between outside and inside. There is no giving and no receiving. There is only movement.

Movement exists because we on Earth believe in time and space. Without time and space there is no movement. The Universe is continually expanding, the scientists tell us. I am continually expanding. We as humans perceive from different source points. Different source points exist because we believe that they do in time and space. We perceive them to be separate in space. Until we don't.

The witness inside us that is eternal can observe our body and mind. In turn, we can observe the witness. We can be the observer of the observer of the observer until there is nothing to observe. And then there is everything. Unlimited possibilities. The Power of *no in and out* offers us infinite possibilities. From the power of infinite possibilities, I choose Peace, Love, Joy, and a hundred other things. What do you choose?

Sacred Technology: Raising the Energy of Power

- **Contract your energy in and expand it out** as big as you can, and then as small. Do this three times. Then move your fingers as if you were expanding in and out. Do this three times. The more slowly and with focus you can do this, the more powerfully your energy will be raised. It is the same energy as a bellows exhaling air into a fire. Notice with your observer witness that you are doing this.

What is the energy of Power? It is joining forces with the Universe and others to think, speak, and act with Peace and Love in the present moment. To walk lightly in the world. To act humbly while simultaneously knowing that all the Power of the Universe is behind you, supporting you. Power comes from the release of a contraction. It is movement directed by our thoughts, words, and the movement of our deeds.

 Power is the activation of manifested thought.

CHAPTER 4

Vow to WOW:
Energy of God Principle

 The external world gives us feedback on how we are doing.

One drop of water has the power of the ocean behind it.

The Chalice

This morning I had a vision about a chalice.

I see a white glass. It is milk glass white. No, it is a chalice. And it is white covered with gold filigree. It looks very rare and important. I see God breathing into the chalice and it overflows. A white misty substance overflows it, running down the sides. Similar to the mist that comes off dry ice. I think that it is way too cold to drink. Then a fire flames across the top and it becomes melted liquid inside.

I think to drink this breath of God that is melted. I drink the substance. It flows down through my body in a circular rolling-down-the-hill motion. It expands out and penetrates my body. Down through my brain and throat and heart and belly and down my legs and out my feet and down my arms and out my hands until every cell is in celebration of receiving the prana that is the breath of God. I am enlightened and illuminated, and yet I am the transformation of the light into form. I already was but now I am renewed as that.

Perhaps I should drink from this chalice every day.

Sacred Technology: Drinking from the Chalice

Drink from the chalice. Try using the above *chalice vision* as a meditation. Read it out loud to yourself or record it. Visualize each sentence as you go.

The God Principle

What do I mean by the God Principle? I can think of a few truths that would apply. Love is the highest form of energy. We are all made of it. Life is God's expression of Love. We can only contact God directly in silence. We have the full support of God for all our needs and desires. The material world offers us feedback on how well we are listening. These are all principles. But *The Principle* is the law or true science of the Universe. This is the science that is beyond the science that we enjoy in the three-dimensional physical world in which we live. That true science comes from beyond the world we live in but exists in this world also. It can override the laws of nature and when it does, we call it miraculous, or magic. Yet it is a divine principle and a kind of law.

Deep Dive into a Bubble

So how do we find the God within? Who am I and how do I discover who I am? This morning I went deep down into my being by descending in a bubble as if I were in a submarine going down deep into the ocean.

> *I think that the ocean is cold. But no, I tell myself I am in a warm bubble. Tiny bubbles drift up from my bubble as I watch myself descend. I stop and here I am in my bubble dressed in a red and gold brocade dress. I have golden hair, and a crown with jewels is on my head.*

I think that this is a bit presumptuous since I am currently dressed in blue jeans that need washing and a tee shirt that says "Teach Ask and Tell." A horse training tee shirt. I also have on a blue work shirt that needs washing. Today is laundry day. But back to descending.

> *I am in this red and gold dress with a crown. Next to me stands Jesus. I ask to hold his hand and he holds my hand. He says that I shouldn't worship him as a person but that I should accept the Christ Consciousness. He seems to disappear, and I descend some more. I am looking for quiet contact with God. I know that it comes from the silence within and so I go deeper.*
>
> *Then I realize that this bubble I am in is the original cell of life force that is divided into many cells, each one containing a replica of the first. With me standing in it. Bubbles continue to rise and I see that the bubbles become each cell that replaces a worn out cell in my body with a perfect replica of a new one and each new one goes to where it is needed, energizing first my chakras: the heart and power and throat. Many enter my throat because they are needed there. My second chakra and brain also get some energizing bubbles. The pineal and pituitary need opening. My body is evolving into a greater spiritual form as these divinely perfect cells spread throughout my body.*
>
> *That original cell was the spark of life. Some call it a star seed or spark of God. I know that it is me. I have contacted my Self and God at this deep level. I am not a servant of God but the daughter. I choose to serve humanity and the universe.*
>
> *Earlier I saw a golden mesh and I was but a joint where lines of gold met. But I can shine out across that mesh so brightly*

> *that my light lights up the universe. I decide to call it back and simply light up the planet earth. Perhaps that is enough for now. That is how I serve humanity. I send forth Peace. I send forth Love.*

I let no thought, word, or deed come through me that is not a *yes*. I only allow what is positively good for humanity. There is no thought of *no* or *I can't* or *lack*. I will not allow those thoughts to enter my being. I see my body as a temple of divine energy. It is like "The Temple of Silence that no hands have made." This temple was described in *Life and Teaching of the Masters of the Far East Vol 1* by Baird T Spalding. Nothing could be chipped away from that temple. It would grow again to repair itself.

I see my body like that. I let no thought that is not Love come through me. I let in only thoughts of Love. *Bad* does not enter here. This is why I entered the depth of myself to contact God. To discover the path forward where only divine perfection and purity of thought can reside. This is how the body returns to the spirit that made it and how it resides in that energy.

> Through this action we can all enter the kingdom of God here on earth and that is already happening. I choose that life.

So where is God inside me? Where do I look? Behind my heart?

God is everywhere in all things, including in all my cells. Every one of them. I don't have to look.

The I Am

Combining Channel Breathing with the Morning Prayer

This morning I decided to combine Dr. Sue Morter's "channel breathing" with my Morning Prayer. I'm getting better at channel breathing. I go about my day while noticing that I can remember to do the channel breath at every breath.

The Morning Prayer words worked perfectly with the channel breathing as I brought in each one and saw them for the energy that they are and I am. Peace, Love, Joy, Beauty, Healing, Harmony, Grace, Communication, Abundance, Gratitude, Magic, Bliss, Truth Divine-Perfection, Co-creation, Power, Glory, Magnificence, Magnitude, Breath, Caring, Freedom, Laughter, Intent, Presence, Purpose, Awareness, Wisdom, and Wonder. Each of these words is an energy that can be felt and danced with. I breathed in *I am that* with each word down and up the central channel in my body.

I saw the energy of *I am* coming in and going into the earth. The energy from the earth was different from the energy of heaven. *In what way? It is slower and heavier.* After a few channel breaths, I decided to stoke the fires with the "breath of fire." I would call it *the bellows breath*. I stoked my fires and then I made the sound of *home*. And I played with the sound that I call my didgeridoo. A few more channel breaths and then I decided to work on some areas of pain.

Breath of Fire into Pain

First my hip. A few channel breaths and then I breathed my hip. A brief remembrance of fear leaving. I stoked the fires seeing the in and out of the energy in the pain point in my hip. I did a few other pain points. Next my left shoulder blade. And then I decided to fire-breathe my left shoulder blade. I did the fire breath as I squeezed into the point of pain. And then I relaxed and hummed it in place. I stoked the fires in several places including my jaw and wrist. The more I noticed, the more pain points appeared for stoking. I did several and then took a deep breath, ran a few channel breaths, and then shook it all out and let out a sigh.

I have for a long time been able to call up any energy like Joy, Peace, or Bliss. Indeed, I can call up any of the energies I list above. What was new this time was the energy of the *I Am*. I saw and felt it going through like a ball of light. Or maybe a little fuzzier, like a stream. I think I have felt separated from it and saw it coming from outside myself instead of coming from me. This gives new meaning to, *to go outside to drop in*.

Now I see inside and outside. And if I give it the *bellows breath*, there will be no difference between the inside and the outside. We exist in both places at the same time.

I Am That

Last night John and I went out for our fifty-second anniversary. We have been dieting so we haven't had any pasta for a while, and I wanted pasta. So we decided to go to Finnelli's in Door County, about an hour away. When we got there, having called and asked for a reservation, which they didn't do, we found that they had moved into Egg Harbor. To Mojo Rose's, a Mexican restaurant. The restaurant had combined three cuisines from three different restaurants in order to stay alive during the COVID-19 pandemic. So, we sat outside under an awning and ordered pasta and carrot cake. We could hear music from a stage in the backyard. We listened for a while and had a cappuccino. The lead guitarist was Mojo's grandson. It was a family affair. We went to bed around 8:30 p.m.—we get up early—and of course I couldn't sleep—too much food so close to going to bed. My stomach rumbled for quite a while.

I decided to meditate.

I ran energy up and down my energy channel. Then I decided to do inching up and down the central channel in both directions. I noticed a few blank spots or tingly spots. I concentrated on them. At one point somewhere between my throat chakra and my third eye, my awareness flipped. I became the energy looking down from above and not the energy going up and out. I stayed there and played with it for a while going back and forth between being the energy rising up and out my crown and the energy going down into my crown. I was both at the same time. I was both the vessel and the energy in the vessel. I had been the energy when I was inching my way up and down. But now I was also the energy up in the sky looking down at the vessel. I inched my way up and down a few more times noticing where the flip occurred. It was somewhere around or in my third eye. I was sure I was in the Cave of Brahmin. Although I don't know what that is. I felt as if I was looking around inside a cave and there were other beings in there with me. But I didn't really care to explore it any further. Then I was up in the sky and looking down. At one point I opened and close my eyes. It didn't seem that there was any difference with my eyes open or closed. I meditated until three or four in the morning. I fell asleep and had a wonderful dream where I flew up into the corner with angel wings and then flew around over water and between buildings. I love flying dreams.

How to Embody Source Energy

Walking Channel Breath

Do the channel breath when you go for a walk or a run. I have adapted this exercise from Dr. Sue Morter's channel breathing, which can be found in her book, *The Energy Codes*.

See your energy running down from above your crown chakra into the earth and back up to the sky. See it as a ball of energy. Know that the ball of energy is your energy. Contract your root chakra, heart chakra, throat chakra and your third eye as you do this. Hold this contraction as you watch the ball of energy rise and fall. Take each breath in as you step on your right foot and exhale out as you step on your left foot. And then switch by bringing the energy up your left foot and out your right foot. If this is too quick, then do it every third or fourth step. Experiment with your own natural walking or running pace and your breathing rhythms.

It is easiest if you match your energy visualization to your breathing as you exercise. You can also match your breathing to your steps. Once you have coordinated your breathing to your steps, then add the visualization of the ball of energy coming up from the earth and ascending into the heavens and returning back down into the center of the earth. If you can't contract all four chakras at the same time, then start with the easiest one. For me that is the root chakra.

You don't have to do a big contraction. You can simply notice or do a tiny squeeze that says, *Hello. How are you?* Then add another chakra by noticing it as you walk along. Eventually you can notice two at the same time. And then three and four. When I do all four, I feel like Sylvester Stallone. I've always wondered where his power came from. He has his chakras pulled back against his spine. You can see it when he walks. Can you walk with the power of Sylvester Stallone?

God Is in All Things

You are God. I am God. You are God. I am God. You are God. I am God. We are God. We are one. United together in thought, word, and action.

It seems somewhat egotistical to think *I am God*. But I remember that I am just a drop of water in the ocean and I have all the power of the ocean behind me. I am humbled because I am just a drop. But I am also emboldened because of the power of the ocean. As children of God, we are simply the drops of *God Ocean*, but we have the power of God behind us.

God is in all things. I exist and therefore God is in me. When I don't resist, I receive more of the God energy that surrounds us all. When I acknowledge it, I consciously do his will, which is heaven on earth right now. All we have to do is accept. Think it and then act on it. *God's will be done.* It seems like I am worshiping God, and I am, but I am not worshiping a male figure holding forth up in the sky. I see God as all-pervasive and residing in all things in all time and space. In fact, he *is* the space and time of all being.

Some speak of the source of all the galaxies and universes as a central sun. Some call it the *Godhead*. I think that our bodies are a similar configuration with our minds being as close as we can get to spirit. Our mind gathers up the God energy and condenses it through our focus and reflects it back out into the world. It returns to us fourfold. So, it behooves us to only send out the vibrations of Love and all the colors, conditions, and tools that make up Love. Like Peace, Joy, Harmony, and Truth. The other lower energies like hate, fear, and doubt also return to us fourfold and cause disharmony like pain and disease. With control of our thoughts, we rule our own lives. We are our own creator of our lives. We should rule them with wisdom and kindness. There is more power in Love than in hate or power over. True Power is in the power of Love, Joy, and Peace.

This time of the year, which is just before the New Year, I am reminded to send out *Peace on earth. Good will toward all men.* I am happy to see that thought return to me fourfold.

Sacred Technology: United with God

Unity with God. Repeat three times: You are God. I am God. You are God. I am God. You are God. I am God. We are God. We are one. United together in thought, word and action.

Hummingbird Wings times Two

I practice the exercise of raising the vibrations of each of my chakras equal to the speed of hummingbird wings. I then ask that each chakra raise its vibration by two times. And then again by two and again by two and again by two. I then ask that all my chakras radiate together and they then also increase by two and by two, until a great, white ray of light emanates from my crown toward the sky. *Is the energy flowing out or is it coming in?* I ask. *It is both.* I send out *Peace on earth. Good will toward men.*

Thrumming

This morning as I considered the hummingbird wings exercise, I thought of the word *thrumming* to describe the exercise. I didn't know if it was a real word. And then that night I read about thrumming in *Druid's Daughter* by Jocelyn A. Fox. *Hmm*, I thought. *Another synchronicity*.

When I thrummed the first and seventh chakras together it was easier than trying for all chakras at once. What happened was that all the chakras in between joined in. And so, focusing on the first and seventh chakras worked out to be easier and more effective.

Then I added sound. I vibrated my lips by putting my top teeth on my bottom lip and making a humming sound. I added that to the vibration of the wings in my chakras. *Now that*, I thought, *is Thrumming*.

Synchronicities

Synchronicities have been happening more and more lately. Especially between John and me. This morning, I thought about flash cards and making them into cards to accompany this book. I wondered whether I should put pictures on both the front and the back, whether I should just use words on one side, and whether or not I should include the animals. Later when John got up and told me of his dream from the night before, he told me about his dream of flash cards and whether he should place them in four categories. He was categorizing the disorders of the mind, like anger and anxiety.

I told him that I was wondering also whether I should create categories for my aspects, conditions, and tools of the

God Principle. So, we were both thinking about flashcards and their pictures and their categories. Coincidence or synchronicity? The more aligned we become, the more synchronicity we experience.

The Conditions: Experiment, Bus Stop, and Time Machines

The Experiment

I was thinking about the conditions of our lives and why we experience the things we do. I considered three different explanations for this. One explanation is called *the experiment*. We (humanity) were put here as an experiment so that we could experience everything that can be experienced and send back a message about our experience, so that God, or the universal intelligence, can experience itself.

The Bus Stop

Or we have Dr. Sue Morter's *bus top conversation* in which she explains that we come into this world with the specific plan to experience something that we had a glimpse of on the way out the last time we were here. And now we want to experience it earlier and have more of that experience. On our way in, we meet others at a bus stop and we chitchat with them. And they say they are willing to help us have a certain experience by playing the other roles that are required for the experience. They are playing the roles of the experience that they need to have for their own selves. Then in we pop and we have forget why we are here but we have that experience. We complain about the experience we are having, not realizing we have chosen it so that we can overcome it. The experience is supporting our growth.

The Time Machine

The third explanation is *the time machine*. Last night I watched the movie *ARQ*. It was a kind of time loop event where the main character keeps repeating his life every time he dies. When he dies, the time resets and he gets to try doing it differently. Since people were trying to kill him, it was important that he find a different way. Each time he tried something different he had a different outcome.

I am reminded of a woman who gets divorced only to remarry the same person over and over again. When will she or any of us learn the lesson we need to learn so that we don't have to repeat it over and over? What if the experience of life is more like the time machine of the *ARQ* movie? Our experience simply resets until we learn to do it differently. Since time is a construct so that we can experience life, we could also see it as a time machine that resets until we change how and what we do.

The point of the *bus stop* is that everything is supporting us and doing so with perfect timing. The point of the *time machine* is that we will continue to repeat our experience until we get it right. And when we do, we just move on to the next right thing. The point of the *experiment* is to simply experience life. Are all three true in their own way? I believe so.

The Inner Alchemist

Before I go to bed, I ask that my inner alchemist transform and transmute all of my cells into newborn baby cells. Those cells have come from the one cell, which has come from the one cell, all the way back to the beginning of the first cell and the start of life on the planet earth. This is the cell of life force energy. It is the cell of God shining his light of love through us. Our life is that Love. How we choose to live it and think about it is a reflection of our acceptance of that Love.

During the morning and throughout the day I give gratitude that my inner alchemist has transmuted my cells, all my cells, my brain, organs, skin, eyes, ears, and throat. All my cells have been transmuted to young and vibrant cells.

As I am washing my hands in the bathroom, I thank my inner alchemist for bestowing beauty and vitality onto me and for having transformed my body so that it can express the love of God through it.

Then I live, laugh, and bless the world. I find Joy in every occurrence that I can. I tell myself that I see it until I can breathe it into being a reality. The energy of the God Principle is consciously recognizing the inner alchemist at work.

 We feel the resistance so that we can go inside ourselves to find ourselves.

CHAPTER 5

How to WOW: Energy of Manifestation

 We create the aspect of our energy by looking at it.

Manifestation: Joy is a tool.

The Shoelace

This morning as I was starting the fire in the fireplace, my shoelace came undone and was in a knot. I struggled for quite some time trying to unknot it. I finally kicked the shoe off to get a better angle on it. I still couldn't get the knot out. I was quite frustrated with it but determined. I couldn't really see it and I could barely feel it. Then I said *BE GONE*. And it was. The knot fell undone in my hands.

I thought about the correct way of saying things. *Be gone*. It's a little like *Behold. The Joy is here.* Or *Behold. I am.* The correct way of saying something is to say it as if it is already done. Say it with gratitude for its being already done. Not *I wish it were so*. Don't continue to ask until you are blue in the face. Ask once and then be grateful that it is done or on its way. How we ask is as important as what we ask.

Manifestation

How do we manifest? How is manifestation related to magic? How does it relate to our abundance? And what is that energy that we call manifestation?

Space: The Final Frontier

We are the space between one energy and the next, and between each of the organized energies that materializes because of the intent of the Universe for us to experience what is and to create what we will experience in the next moment. We also reside in that potentiality.

Before this morning, I clung to the idea that energy was like liquefied matter. And that energy permeated through our bodies, which are energy densified. Are we this energy? Yes. But we are also the space between that which organizes the energies. We organize energy around and through the densified particles. We do this to the extent that they are particles at all. But we call them matter anyway.

Trees don't put their roots into the earth. They actually put their roots into the space between the so-called particles of earth. We don't actually contact the earth with our feet if we are barefoot. We float on a tiny layer of energy between us and the earth.

The space between where all the organized energy flows is where we find unity. It is also where time doesn't exist. Infinite possibility exists there. That is why I call it *the final frontier* like in the television series, *Star Trek*.

The Bridge

We act as the bridge between the Mother Mary energy of the ninth chakra two feet above our heads and the Christ Consciousness energy of the tenth chakra, which is one foot below our feet. I can't help but think of the phrase *the Father, the Son, and the Holy Spirit*. But no, that doesn't work for me. It is male energy and female energy, and we are the bridge between. We are the child energy.

We are the harmony that occurs when the creative male force harmonizes with the nurturing female force. We as humans create a new world, a new consciousness, from that place. We have the senses to feel and taste. *That feels good* or *that tastes bad* are our experiences. From our experiences we can intend something new and better. From our intentions we create it.

Intent fluctuates the breath of the universe.

Intention

Intent fluctuates the breath of the universe, which sends billions of photons of information down into our beings and particularly into where our bellies are located, the seat of our wisdom. Our gut intuition. Our brain organizes and focuses some of the information into useful bits. Our ego brain tries to protect us. Our hearts soften the organization into softer awareness energy. Awareness expands our focus. Power is focused energy. Our intention when focused is powerful. Intention grabs our attention and our focus. Our will sustains our focus. Will is empowered by practice, exercise, and habit. Some would call this combination *discipline*.

Attraction

What we focus on is where we send our energy and our attraction. The law of attraction is not so much about attracting an energy as it about changing our perception of what we see in the world. What we perceive we become. When we become an energy like Peace, we see more Peace in the world. We are looking at the world from a different place and we no longer see so much struggle and overwhelm. Some say that we have stepped into a new dimension. We each live in our own dimension. All the other players are in their own dimensions. They may see something else. They always will.

Perception

But what is the perception from space? From the spaces between all energies. Space is infinite potentiality. Our intent enters that space and is birthed into reality. It first becomes energy and then becomes matter. Infinite potentiality is who we truly are. The space of intention. From there we have a choice about which energies to move around and send or bring into our bodies. To experience the world we are living in, it helps if we see ourselves as embodied energy. We are both inside our bodies and outside our bodies at the same time. But we only experience from inside our bodies. We need to stay there.

Sacred Technology: Experience Embodiment

Embody your energy. Sit your awareness in your lower three chakras. Breathe in and out from a place in each of the three lower chakras. See a ball of light expanding and contracting with your breath. In and out three times in each chakra. Contract the root chakra up into the pelvic bowl and breathe in and out from the second chakra. Contract in as far as you can and then breathe out as far as you can from chakras two and three. Then let out a sigh; make it audible. This will integrate that energy into your physical body.

No Real Understanding

For several years, I have given away ever understanding the idea that the why and how of many things can't be understood or known, so I told myself, *Don't try to figure it out.* In the meantime, I accepted what is and moved on. My understanding was that there is no real understanding. *Understanding* has never been one of my words, the words that I categorized into the aspects, conditions, and tools of divine God energy. Maybe *understanding* should be one of my tools.

Today I read about a rishi's explanation of Solomon and his being given the gift of *understanding;* that gift was the reason he was so wise. I don't know the truth of that occurrence, but it has led me to question whether or not we can understand the order of the Universe and our lives in it. After all, isn't that what my writing is all about? Aren't these possible explanations for the laws of energy and the universal principles of life as I see them played out before me. As I journey myself through experiencing many understandings, some I accept as explanations and some I accept as events that will never be understood.

Already Done

Today I tried to understand the sixth principle of Rikka Zimmerman's *Six Principles*. That IT is already done. A complete listing of the six principles can be found in the resources at the back of this book.

Last Thursday, I began the conversation about *already done* with my friend Leslie regarding healing—that a healing is already done by the time a person asks for it. So, I said, "Why do we as Life Coaches go through all this talk about everything? Why lead people through a process or take hours, weeks, and years, when it can be done with the snap of a finger or a touch or just the thought of a touch? When essentially it is already done? With a touch. And even before the touch, it is already done. The person is whole and complete."

Whole and complete happens to be Rikka's second principle.

It is a little like when you call on your guide and discover that he is already here. All we have to do is begin to want something and it is already here. It is the same way with healing all things. When healing another, that person must want to be healed, must want to be whole. I choose to use *whole* instead of *healed* because there seems to be less judgment about being broken in the first place if we can become *whole* as opposed to *healed*. The person has to believe that they will be made whole.

The energy of the healer raises the energy of the person high enough that they are in direct contact with the divine healing energy of God. And if they choose it, they are made whole. It is already done from the healer's perspective and instantaneous from the other person's perspective, if they choose it.

Manifesting and Already Done

This morning I was also considering *already done* from a manifestation standpoint. It can seem somewhat incongruous when one is wishing for a different outcome or for something to take place or to have something appear in their life and to also think that it is already done. Obviously, it isn't, or they wouldn't be wishing for it. The usual answer to this dilemma is that you haven't truly wished for it because you have stopped it from happening. Then you blame yourself for not wishing strongly enough or imagining clearly enough or whatever else you want to blame yourself for. What we focus on draws our energy to it. So, stop focusing on what isn't there and focus on what is there and be grateful for what is.

Don't even be grateful for what is coming. It will just continue to be coming and never arrive.

The Universe is like a servant who fills the cup of his master before he even asks. Or a waiter who fills your glass of iced tea before you ask. I have experienced one of those waitresses at Red Lobster. Her name is Michelle. I always ask for her when I go there because she always watches and replenishes. Like that, the Universe is watching and replenishing. It sees where our focus is. And then it replenishes and shows up answering our focus.

So *already done* follows our desire and our focus, or our attention, and responds almost instantaneously. Before we can get the words out. So that is why our words should be *thank you for being here*. *Thank you* for this iced tea or this loaf of bread. Thank you, God, for this bountiful abundance that gives me this loaf of bread. This chocolate ice cream, this bowl of strawberries or this thousand dollars or this new car. Thank you for my good health. For this life on this earth. Thank you for my understanding of *already done*.

Dream: Magic

> *I am in the center of a group of people. I ask what their ailment is. They tell me and then I take action. I ask them a few questions and they are slowly healed. I heal them one at a time.*

> *Then I notice that they are in a circle and I am in the center of the circle. I begin to slowly spin around as I stand in the center of the group. I reach out to each of them pointing my finger at them as I spin by. I stop spinning. Then I hold my hands up above my head like a flamenco dancer. And I decide to make the sound of bells ringing. Small bells like tiny fairy bells. They more tinkle than ring. I ask the people if*

they would like to hear the bells and they say yes. So I start to tinkle them. Each tiny bell tinkles as I move my fingers until many bells are tinkling at the same time. Eventually, the people fall asleep as they listen to the bells. They surround me sleeping in a circle, lying on couches and chairs.

I turn away from the group and look outside. I see a balcony. Then I jump off the balcony and land lightly on the ground. I turn back to see a woman who is standing on the balcony and I tell her that she can also jump and land safely on the ground. I tell her that it is easy and that she can also do this. She says no; she will just walk down the stairs and go around.

Then I decide to fly up into the corner of a room. But there is no room. So I just fly up into the sky. I stay there and look back down like Wonder Woman when she is fighting Ares. I turn to look down at a car. The people in the car look up at me with surprise. I hold my position in the air. I decide that it is time to fly into the corner of a room and hold my position there. I look down from a corner of a ceiling. I have always wanted to do that. How magical, I think, and then I wake up to the remembrance of the magic that was in my dream and still is.

What It Means

The dream reminds me to remember that the magic that is in the world surrounds us. My morning meditation word today was *Gratitude*. I am grateful to remember that gratitude is the catalyst for all magic and to bring more magic into the world, we need to be grateful for what already exists. What already exists is a magical world. And I am grateful for that.

The Energy of Magic

What is the energy of Magic? It is the energy of *anything is possible* and *I don't know what will happen next*. It is the energy of *how did this happen?* It is the energy of a miracle or an unexplained cosmic coincidence. It occurs when our spiritual energy is perfectly aligned with the spiritual energy of the Universe. And then we notice that something magical is happening in front of us.

Magic is always happening in front of us. But we don't notice it unless we are aligned with the energy that surrounds us. Gratitude is a huge catalyst for it to occur. Gratitude is a catalyst because it aligns our energy with the energy that surrounds us. When we are grateful for our surroundings and what exists, we are aligned with that energy. We become that energy. When we become that energy, we are perfectly aligned with the Universe. That alignment creates the magic.

The gratitude for what already exists allows the universe to set up what we want to occur. The gratitude takes us out of the energy of wanting into the energy of loving what we already have. That grateful energy says to the Universe, *Yes. And I would like even more. You decide what dessert will be.* Then the Universe offers us chocolate ice cream. And we call it magic. Magic is the dessert that the Universe offers us. I say, "Eat dessert first. Life is uncertain." Yes, life is uncertain. But I also say it is the uncertainty that gives us the magic. Magic is also the energy of uncertainty. If it were certain, it would be the energy of reason. The energy of reason is not the energy of magic. Magic is unreasonable. And that is a good thing!

Sacred Technology: Experience More Magic

- **Choose magic.** Say three times: *I choose to see the magic that already exists in the world.*
- **Give gratitude for magic.** Say three times: *I am grateful for the magic that already exists in the world.*

No Need to Need

I had a dream a couple of nights ago where …

Dream

> *I place my hands on a person's head. One hand on each side and I heal them. Then I scoot my butt across the room. I am half levitating and scooting, and then I fly up into a corner of the room. I come back down to sit next to Rikka. We chat and I seem to be looking for her approval. She scoots away from me on the bench. I scoot over closer to her and then she scoots over to another bench. I am congratulating myself for finally flying up into the corner of the room. It is an action that I have been trying to do and have done several times. I am pleased with myself. But I don't quite understand Rikka's reaction.*

I was talking to my friend Leslie yesterday. I told her about my dream, and we discussed people's need for approval. We both shared instances where we were looking for approval. True approval has to come from within. It cannot come from outside us. There is a resistance that happens when someone comes up to us and desperately wants our approval. Many times, we turn away from them, citing some reason, such as we don't approve. Or we give them our approval even if we don't mean it. They turn away never satisfied with or without our approval, because the real approval has to come from inside themselves. Looking at the need for approval turned me to looking at needing, and the need for need.

I looked at the need for need. It is a lot like the resistance to resistance. When we resist something, it stays around longer than when we just let it go. So how do we stop resisting resistance? We let it all go. It is the same with need. How do we not need to need? We let it go. We simply let go of the need for need. Do I need approval. Yes. I think there was a bit of need there. Approval has to be something that we can receive or not receive, and it doesn't matter. Thank you for your approval and Thank you for your disapproval. It doesn't matter. Only when it doesn't matter can we truly move on. That's what I mean by letting it go—making it not matter.

Move on to what? Move on to the next true thing on our path. But path to where? I guess it's just the path home to ourselves. Which is where we already are. Nowhere to go. We should simply enjoy where we are.

Sacred Technology: Let Go of the Need for Approval

- **Need for approval.** Let go of the need for approval. Let go of the need for anything. Allow it to be okay if you get approval or you don't get approval. Approve of yourself for letting go of the need for approval. You can fill in the blank with any need you have.
- **No need.** Then let go of the need for need. How? Just say *I now let go of the need for needing*.

Spreading Peace

I have been playing with the energy of Peace. It is one of the colors or energies of God, Source. Even if we hold or have Peace inside us, we can't project it out. That is not the way to offer peace to the world. Or spread our peace if we find we have it and want to share it. I have chosen to hold and share it with the world right now because I believe the world could use some Peace energy right now.

So how does spreading peace occur? It radiates out from the individual who has so much peace inside them that it overflows and leaks out. It radiates out when we have that much peace. We don't really gather it up and send it out. We simply are it and it radiates out. How do we become it? We become it by seeing Peace in all things around us. If we don't see it, we can ask to be shown the Peace that surrounds us. And when we ask that, we are shown it. When Peace is what we see, then Peace is what exists. It shines forth as we interact with all that surrounds us. When we look at two people seeming to have an argument and we stand in Peace, the argument stops. They will turn to look at us. Maybe even forgetting what they were arguing about. Or maybe it no longer is so important. When we stand in Peace, we are no longer able to argue with ourselves. We simply step forward and take the right action. How do we know it is the right action? Because we are at Peace.

This may seem like circular reasoning. But it is the nature of co-creation. We choose and then we become what we choose. And then we choose from what we have become. It is both a self-fulfilling prophesy and a chicken-and-egg phenomenon.

The energy of manifestation is allowance, gratitude, and celebration. This is the tool I call *Joyfinity*. It is aligning your body, mind, and spirit with all that is. And then asking once for what you can't quite need because it is already here, manifested.

 The external world gives us feedback on how we are doing.

CHAPTER 6

Here and WOW: Energy of Transmuting

 Fighting and getting angry show a lack of self-love.

How do you get all of this into your physical body? Inspiration and Infusion

Teaching and Flowers

> Light workers are putting their classes on computer screens. There are many people and they are trying to let the world know about their classes through advertising and branding. Then Rikka shows up and pulls them all after her down the street.
>
> I turn to look at some flowers. I think they are mine and I notice they are in pots. I think I should take them with me. Then I look closer. They are planted in the ground and they are Rikka's flowers. They are next to a stage where she speaks. They landscape her stage in a beautiful way. Then I think, "No. These are her flowers, and I will get my own flowers."

When I remembered this morning's dream, I thought that we each need to get our own flowers and plant them so they will grow and beautify our stages. We cannot take another's flowers. These flowers express our own individual, beautiful way of being.

Higher and Lower Frequencies

What we think of as positive or negative energy, I would call higher energy frequencies or lower energy frequencies. Or I might call them contractive energies or expansive energies. *Negative* is such a negative word. It assumes a judgment about energy when energy is just energy. It is neither good nor bad. It is one frequency or another and it is either expansive or contractive. Or it is a higher frequency or a lower frequency.

We call certain energies like hate, greed, or anger negative because their frequencies are low. Other energies like love, peace, and joy are called high energies. Love is the highest frequency. Joy is also very high. We tend to call hate a low energy. But these so-called low energies can also be considered contractive energies. And when we expand, we also need to contract. We could also call those contractive frequencies grounding frequencies. We can either choose to physically contract and ground our energy consciously or our bodies will contract our energy for us by offering us hate, shame, and greed. Or we might contract our energies by overstuffing our bodies with food or watching too many action-based shows on television.

Where we place out attention, there goes our energy. Consciously practicing exercises that contract or ground our energy can lessen the need for our bodies to contract us into anger in order to balance the expansion we have been feeling when we practice Love, Joy, and Peace. Many of the exercises in this chapter will help to contract the body so that we don't have to drop into the lower frequency emotions to balance our expansions.

Pet Peeves and Unity

I was thinking about my pet peeves with other people who are constantly on their cell phones in every waking moment. Particularly my husband, John. I try to dismiss it and allow it because there is really nothing I can do to change it. But it still bugs me. Then I thought about the words *pet peeve*. Why would we make a peeve into something that we would keep as a pet? Or why would we stroke it? Do we want to antagonize ourselves so much that we can't stand it anymore and then we do something about it? At first, I thought the answer was no. But now I realize that is exactly what we are doing. We are giving ourselves a strong experience. And every experience we come across is a gift to ourselves. We experience our pet peeves because they emit a strong reaction in us.

Sometimes we walk away from something we cannot stand. Sometimes we confront it because we think we can change it, and sometimes we *can* change it. Other times we try to ignore it or endure it. But why is it happening in the first place and why does it make a difference? It is there because some part of us on the inside is separated from the whole and asks for it to be there. Until we resolve the split inside ourselves, we will continue to see the split outside us.

But how do we resolve the split inside us? We look inside and ask, *Where are you?* Then we breathe into that spot and send it love or at least we love that spot. You will find there is a contraction, or a density, there. Release and relax that spot. You might think of Peace at that spot. Once it is peaceful, you can expand that spot and send it love. You are already sending it Love by placing your attention there.

Pet peeves are really gifts we give ourselves to know where in ourselves we are divided and not whole. Some would say we are not unified.

Another person behaving *badly* is simply playing out something that is disconnected inside us. Once we connect it, the need for the other person to behave in a certain way changes. It is always about us and rarely about the other person. When we are whole, the other person finds that they no longer behave in a certain way. Our pet peeves always support us.

When we are no longer running away from something, or trying to change something, then we are whole in that regard. There will always be something new to consider.

The more we step into Love, the less we react to what is going on around us, and the more we proactively create the world we wish to see. And the more that world shows up for us to experience. All these conditions are collectively bringing us into ourselves.

Unity happens when we give up living in a dualistic world and choose to step forward into a loving world where all decisions are made from Love and the colors of Love like Peace and Joy.

So to those on their cell phones in my presence, I say, *Thank you for disregarding me!* Now I can simply regard myself and let you be yourself.

Authenticity

If we behave one way with one group of people and differently with another group, then we are acting out two different parts of ourselves. If we behave the same way in both situations or in front of both groups, then we are behaving authentically. Authenticity is our goal, stemmed from oneness. Our goal is to behave authentically in all situations. Behavior can be appropriate to different situations but still be authentic to the individual. I might speak differently to a child than I would to an adult. But I can still be authentic to both.

You can stand strong, have values, and still love everyone. Don't try to drive yourself to Love. You can't make yourself love someone you don't love. When you love someone you previously didn't agree with, it should surprise you. It should just happen, all of a sudden, that you notice you can love that person. Then the Love is authentic. Return the power you might have used to fight the other person, or to drive your love to another person, toward loving yourself. Direct your power inward. Allow your love to blossom and grow. Blossoming and growing is authentic.

Sacred Technology: Resolving the Split

- **Inside and Outside.** Look at something or someone outside yourself. Now pull your awareness inside yourself. Look outside. Now inside. Go back and forth increasing the speed until there is no difference between outside and inside. And you are one with the outside and inside.

The Wave Action: Anger, Fear, and Peace

Anger and Fear

This morning I thought about anger. I know that it gets you up off the couch to do something. I know that it can be a great motivator. It also anchors us. I can see that we are pulled into our body with anger, until we release it. We should release it with an expansion. Positive energies are expansive. In order to expand, do we have to contract? Yes, because contraction and expansion create a wave action. Only Source can continually expand without a contraction. But some say, even there, there is a contraction going on.

In occupying matter, we have to contract to expand. Are they equal and opposite? Not necessarily. The jellyfish contracts a little and then shoots forward. When we swim, we

Attract what you *do* want.

contract to move forward and then we expand out to grab some more water to propel ourselves forward.

Anger anchors or contracts us so that we can move forward with delight and Joy or whatever other positive energy or emotion we choose. It could be Peace or Love.

Choose Peace

I am the expert of nothing. That is funny to be an expert of nothing. Nobody is an expert at nothing and by that logic, I am nobody. So, I am nobody and I am an expert at nothing. From that place of nothing is where I choose something. Some call that place the *heart of God* or *zero point*, or simply nothing. What do I choose? Today I choose Peace. I choose to be Peace.

I think that the world needs Peace. The present turmoil of shootings, Covid-19, and the fires and storms mean that many people are afraid and contracted. Although actually, I don't believe they are in their bodies—they are focused on the fear outside themselves. They are attached to the fear and anger that is scattered around the world. They have left pieces of themselves out there with that attachment. There is much anger.

I will not leave myself scattered out there. I am aware of it but I will reside in myself with Peace. I will be Peace. I choose Peace. *Nothing* is a very good place from which to choose any high energy. I love being the expert of nothing!

Sacred Technology: Choose Peace

- **Be the peace you want to see in the world.** Call up the energy of Peace. Infuse it into every cell of your body. Breathe peace in and out. Breathe peace into all of your chakras one at a time. Breathe peace out through your heart chakra to the world. Stand in that place throughout your day.

Peace and Black Lives Matter

Peace is simply a color of Love. There is such unrest in the world. The US is burning in several cities across the country where rioters and protesters have marched and burned buildings in the nights following the death of George Floyd. It was shown clearly on a video, where a black man was killed by a white policeman while he screamed, "I can't breathe."

The unjust treatment of minorities has been rampant throughout all the institutionalized systems in this country: healthcare, justice, education, and employment. Right now, there are two pandemics, Covid-19 and the injustice of racism against minorities.

All lives matter. Black lives, brown lives, yellow lives, white lives, and blue lives. People are marching in protest. Some protestors created destruction because they wanted to be heard. They believe peaceful people are not heard. Because they haven't been heard. But for real change to occur, there must be peace.

Peace comes from respect. Minorities need to be treated with respect. We need to respect all people. We also need to respect all levels of our governments and those who work in them. We need to trust our governments and we need to change what is not working. We need to improve things. All things can be improved. There needs to be enough respect toward everyone so we can listen to each other. The police need to respect those they are protecting and helping. The community needs to respect those who protect them. Peace begins with respect, trust, and justice.

Threats of force only escalate a bad situation. Protection needs control. Real control only comes from a sense of fairness and justice. Peace occurs in this place of trust and fairness. Control can only be pasted on a situation like a band aid. It will come off and the underlying hurt needs to be healed or it will flare up.

Peace is a color of Love. Love consists of all the colors of the rainbow. There is a lesson in that. So many religions and cultures have descriptions of rainbows followed by Peace. Peace with a dove carrying an olive branch. What olive branch can be given to the oppressed who are currently in such great pain? The olive branch needs to be in all areas. In education, criminal justice, healthcare, and employment. We need to love our fellow man. Regardless of color or age or race or gender orientation.

Peace is simply a color of Love. All lives matter. Black lives, brown lives, yellow lives, white lives, and blue lives.

Sacred Technology: Peace at Bedtime

- **Notice peace.** When you go to bed, ask yourself, *How did my day change because I was Peace. What did I notice?*

Clouds

I sat with my coffee this morning, looking up at the clouds. I thought about Wayne Dyer writing in *Your Sacred Self* about his playing with the clouds with his children. He talked about making animals out of the clouds as they passed overhead, and he and his children made a game out of it to see who could make the best shapes out of the clouds. He used this as an example of practicing our ability to interact with our surroundings.

Revealing What's Underneath

There were a lot of clouds this morning, so I decided to see what shapes showed up. I saw a bunny and then two bunnies. They were lying on their sides as if nursing from their mother. One bunny slowly shifted into a puppy and the other passed by overhead and was lost from my sight as it floated over the leaves of the maple tree off my deck.

I thought, *I'm not making the shapes. The shapes are revealed to me in their passing just as Michelangelo sculpted away the excess marble in his sculptures.* He said, "The sculpture is already complete within the marble block, before I start my work. It is already there, I just have to chisel away the superfluous material." I was only seeing what was already there in the clouds. I wasn't creating it.

Wayne Dyer spoke of trying to create the shapes. We don't really create them. We just acknowledge them as they show up. We don't create our reality as much as we chip away at the excess and see what is already there underneath.

We let go of the excess junk that we carry around, like hate and fear. Fear of not being good enough or fear of not being loved. When we let go of that junk, we see what is already there hiding underneath: that we are already good enough and that we are already loved and loving. What if we could simply sculpt ourselves like Michelangelo and discover that divine perfection that awaits us underneath?

Sacred Technology: Interacting with the Energy of Clouds

- **Cloud energy.** Watch the clouds as they pass overhead. See what shapes appear. Are you creating them or are they already there and you are simply noticing and recognizing what is there?

Sacred Technology: Giant Bubbles for Cleansing and Awareness

- **Giant bubbles.** Imagine that you have a giant bubble wand and are pulling a huge bubble up from your feet over your entire body. It is the kind of bubble that you see at fairs. The small ones come out of a bottle. The large ones come out of a bucket.
- **Start with a red bubble** and pull it from below your feet to above your head. When you get to the top of your head, the bubble forms a fine mesh, like a screen. It is no longer a long bubble but a flat circular screen.

As the bubble flattens it gathers all of the clinkers that it encounters as it moves through your body and then pops them out into the universe where they are dissolved. These clinkers are the *fear* and *not safe* that are stored in your root chakra and have spread throughout your body.

- **Next create another bubble**. This one is orange. Feel it surround your entire body and pull it way above your head with your wand. Pull it all the way through your body and watch as it snaps into a flat solid orange screen above your head. The disc has gathered slightly smaller chunks of stuff. They might be bits of *I am not so creative*. You don't have to know what they are to get rid of them. Just notice them and let them go.

- **Next create a yellow bubble.** This bubble is even more refined. Pull it through like the others. Allow it to solidify above your head. Notice the debris that is released into the universe as it solidifies. This will clear the debris around your beliefs about your personal power. Your misbeliefs of *I am not enough*.

- **Next create a giant green bubble** and bring it through your body. Even more refined than the previous bubble, it too snaps together as a solid screen above your head. Notice it throwing out any emotions of not being loved or being incapable of loving.

- **Then create a pink bubble** for your high heart chakra. This will clear from anywhere in your body anything blocking the idea of your being Love.

Notice as the pink disc throws out even more refined debris.

When I first did this exercise, I noticed that curled-up human beings were being flung from my body. I was surprised. It wasn't just a fine dust. There were curled-up beings of my alter egos, which I had been storing in my heart. I let them go. Whatever is being brought up just allow it to leave. You don't have to understand it or analyze it.

- **Next create a blue bubble**. Bring it around your entire body starting at your feet and pull it over your head. This will clear out your throat chakra and allow you to speak and hear more clearly.

  Again, with this exercise I had whole beings—like people—being removed from my system. I let them go. You are just as likely to find refined dust leaving or large pieces of junk. I usually think of the bubble mesh as getting more refined as I go up the chakras. I think that the grosser mesh catches the bigger pieces, and the more refined meshes catch the smaller pieces. But this is just my mind organizing the colors and the mesh sizes. So, I also see entire beings leaving with the more refined pieces. Whatever happens, allow it. Allow what wants to leave to leave.

- **Go to your third eye chakra** and use an indigo bubble to clear your body. Pull it up around your body and out over your head. Watch what leaves as it solidifies into a disc way above your head.

- **Create a lavender bubble** for your crown chakra and pull it over your entire body from your feet to your head. Watch what leaves.
- **Now, reverse the direction of the bubbles**. Pull a golden bubble down from above your head to down below your feet. Then follow with a white bubble. Notice what leaves. Watch as whatever leaves dissolves into the earth.
- **Feel the energy** that occupies the space of your body cleansed and aware. Do this practice once a week or as often as you feel sluggish.

> *Your dreams give you feedback on how you are doing in both worlds.*

Letting Go of Dreams

Last night I had the most amazing experience. I went to bed early as I always do. I read for a little while and then proceeded to go to sleep. As I lay there nodding off, I thought about the yard beside the garage at my parents' house on Broadway. I couldn't see the yard. But I saw it the way I see it in my dreams. And then my dreams started floating in. I was amazed as I watched them—visions of scenes I had previously had in hundreds of dreams. I asked myself, *And what other dreams did I have?* I don't usually remember my dreams.

Only on occasion do I remember a dream. I tell myself to remember it if it is a good or a magical one. I don't remember the ones where I am scared or running away from something. Now this morning upon awakening, I have access to all of them. Then I switched over to all the dreams I had at my grandparents' house in Antigo. There were hundreds there also. And I asked *Can I see my skating dreams? Are there any that I need to look at?* There were several there also.

This morning I still have access to all of them. I asked, *Why is this so?* Last night, when all my memories were floating in front of my eyes, I thought perhaps I was dying. After all you hear that when you are about to die your whole life floats in front of you. But no, I wasn't exactly dying. I was dying to my dreams that were full of fear and struggling. I was simply dying to them.

This morning I asked, *Why has this happened?* I was told that this was a way to bring the scary and struggling dreams into the light. So that I could let go of them or transform them into the light. There were so many dark shadows and ghosts lurking outside windows and doors. And along streets and sidewalks that I traveled down. And car rides and bus rides that I took, all running away from some dark unknown. Today I let them all go in one *swell foop*!

I think I was actually letting them go last night. I asked to see some of the positive and magical dreams, but I didn't seem to want to go there. Just the scary and dark dreams. But they were no longer scary and dark. They just were. A transformation occurred.

Why did this happen? I had asked to be shed of all my worry and anxiety. All of my fears and struggle. I had prayed to the God within me to let them go so that I could shine forth my light to spread Peace, Love, and Joy on the earth. Perhaps this was my answer, a preparation for doing that.

The world is always in balance. When we expand we need to contract. In order to go high into the heavens, we have to have our feet firmly planted on the earth. The more we raise our energy frequencies, the more grounded we have to be. The grounding and contracting energies are not bad. They are useful. Use them until they are no longer needed. Then let them go or rename them. They are just energy.

> *The same energy that causes the revolt causes the bliss. You choose.*

CHAPTER 7

Now to WOW: Purity of Energy

 The moment we have everything, we need to move forward.

Everything is Energy

We each have the ability to live our lives obeying the rules of energy. In fact, we already do whether we are conscious of it or not. Easy and fast is living by the rules consciously. Shift your internal GPS to the rules of energy.

Portals

I started playing with portals a few years ago. I was sitting at a friend's lake home in Northern Wisconsin. I was on the deck looking out at the forest in front of me. The trees were so thick that they almost obscured the lake. When I looked up into the trees, I saw wheels of energy. The wheels were like concentric circles. They didn't last long. At first, I thought that it was the energy of the tree that I was seeing. And in a way it was. But it was also something else. Since then, I have seen the wheels many times and most recently, I have begun playing with them.

I believe the wheels to be portals. *So why not go inside them?* I ask myself. *But how do I do this?* They seem to disappear so quickly. They sit in my awareness and then I notice them. If I try to hold them, they disappear. So, interacting is about allowance and just allowing them to show up. I couldn't decide if I should say *interacting* or *inneracting*. That is so funny, because both are true.

Pure Energy

Pure energy is without a name. It is neither good nor bad, yet we try to define it, to make it recognizable and useful. To use it, we need to claim it, categorize it, and give it a name. But no matter what we call it, it is just pure energy. Energy has rules such as it has to move and can't be contained. I first wrote about these in my book, *Absolute Joy*. You can find the rules of energy in the appendix section at the back of this book.

Allow and Notice

I practice allow and notice. *Allow, notice. Allow, notice.* Take a deep breath and exhale. Just look around. Forget about everything. When you look around eventually, the portals will show up. And then say, "Oh, there you are." Say *thank you* and let it be. When they disappear, don't try to hang on to them. They will return sooner if you haven't contracted your energy by trying to hang on to them.

This morning during my meditation, the wheels showed up in two trees in front of my deck. I simply noticed them and allowed them. But today, the wheels started to change. They spiraled and combined. So, I thought, *Why not join them?* Then I thought that, if they were portals, they would act like the gates in the science fiction series, *Stargate*. And that there would be a portal on this side and also one on the other side.

Since there are an infinite number of portals and they are everywhere, one would have to choose the portal here and also choose the portal on the other side. One could simply join the two portals in a kind of spiral, like a yin and yang. You could join them forward or backward in time or in different locations. This would be a way to jump from one location to another.

I had previously played with noticing the portals behind me. After all you don't really see them with your eyes. You see them with your mind's eye, or your "inner eye" as my friend Christine Laria likes to call it. So, I am capable of noticing the portals behind me as well. I previously thought that rather than stepping forward through the portals. I would step backwards through one, or perhaps I would just turn around and look at myself as I sat in one that was behind me. The portals are all around us infinitely. So where is the portal that I am currently residing in?

Jumping In

I can't see myself as a tunnel or as a flat wheel with a tunnel emanating from it. So, I see myself as a ball. I think that I have to join my ball with what I am perceiving as a tunnel behind a flat gate. But that doesn't seem right. Instead, I can perceive myself as a large chakra. First, I see the seven chakras in the human body as gates. Then I see one big chakra. I don't know if I have combined them or if my heart or crown chakra has taken over. Maybe my third eye has taken over because, after all, this practice is about perception.

"Taken over" feels a little unsafe so I remind my root chakra that it gets to come along also.

At some point I will join my very large chakra gate to the one I perceive and jump. Oops! I already have. The chakra gates have combined.

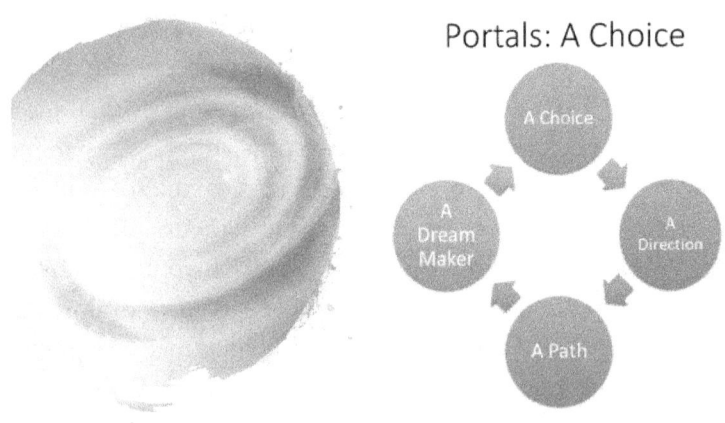

Portals: A Choice

A Cosmic Coincidence of Portals

I was sitting in my living room talking to my husband, John, this morning. I was telling him about my morning meditation and the wheels. He said, "Funny you should say that. This morning I dreamed that I was in Kentucky. And there was this wheel in front of me and I could see Minneapolis on the other side like it was on a screen. So, I floated up and became a jet plane and flew to Minneapolis. I snapped back a few times. I could see people and places on the tunnel walls. But they were all fuzzy. And I could hear the control tower talking. They said, 'But you can't possibly be here now, because you only left Kentucky four minutes ago.' "

I laughed. John was having this dream at the same time I was having and writing about my experience from this morning's meditation. This is one of the many cosmic coincidences we have.

Sacred Technologies for Activating Our Perception of the Portals

- **Practice "Allow and Notice."** Take a deep breath and exhale. Just look around. Forget about it all. When you look around, eventually, the portals will show up. And then say, "Oh, there you are." Say, *Thank you* and let it be. When they disappear, don't try to hang on to them. They will return sooner if you aren't contracted by trying to hang on to them. Notice them and allow them to appear and disappear. Allow them to show up. Notice when you notice that they show up. Breathe and relax and let them all go. Then notice. Don't look for them. Just Notice.

- **Practice switching between fuzzy awareness and focus.** Doing this will help with the above practice. Awareness is fuzzy. Let all focus go from your awareness and watch the world from your peripheral vision. Then focus your eyes intently on an object. Like a chair or a rock in front of you. Go back and forth between awareness and focus. Increase this more and more rapidly until they seem to combine. When they combine, then you will be able to do both at the same time.

The advantage of this is that you can move forward when you focus. This is where you place your attention. And this is your intention. Awareness is the place where you discover infinite possibilities. And from this place you can select where you want to place your focus. You need both possibility and choice. Possibility (fuzzy) offers you the choice whereas making the choice (focus) moves you forward. Awareness and focus experienced together at the same time increase your energy and power.

Energy and Understanding

Dancing and Seeing Energy

Many years ago, I asked to see energy. I thought it would look like colors floating in space or surrounding everything. And in a way it does. I do see it. At the time I screamed at the Universe that I wanted to see energy. My guides laughed at me and said that there was nothing wrong with their ears and that I should try whispering. And then I learned to whisper. I learned that whispering was not only heard by the Universe, but it was even more powerful. This is how I came up with the power and lightness exercise described in chapter 3. I have also learned that in dancing with energy and weaving energy, the lightest touch is also the most powerful.

> *I bring energy down around and through the space around my body. I wave my hands at it. I can slice it open and enter into it. Or beckon out what's in there. I can raise my hand up to the sky and explode the energy into a million sparkles of light.*
>
> *But I can also just move the tip of my finger a tiny bit and create something even more powerful.*

We *see* energy in many different ways. I see it with my third eye as it dances. And I feel it. It moves me and I move it. I call this dancing. When I move it with intention, I call that weaving. I also call it *seeing* energy. It isn't just like seeing a movie because that is more passive. Or maybe it is because a movie isn't real. It is in the realm of the imagination. And energy is definitely something that our imagination fosters. Our imagination creates dreamtime, which creates our dreaming consciousness, which creates our world that we have chosen to live in consciously or unconsciously. I choose to live in it consciously.

Better Understanding

For the last few days, I have asked the Universe to double my brain capacity. We only use 10 percent of our brains. I want to use 20 percent. At least as a starter. Dolphins use 20 percent. It's not that I want to swim in the ocean or use sound vibrations, although that would be fun. It's that I wish to better understand the world we live in. Understanding is such a silly concept. How can we understand the "not understandable"? But I believe with a greater brain capacity, I would have a better understanding. So I ask.

Bilocating as Energy

Bilocation is a matter of perception. I perceive myself as being over there and then bilocate to over there. I turn around and look back. What do I see but myself in another place where I first started? So, I tell myself, *Pull all my selves back to me—clean, clear, and abundant.* This is something I do whenever I am feeling split apart or all over the place. When I feel scattered. This happens when you multitask and are not present in this moment and in this place. It also happens every time you interact with someone. You leave a piece of yourself with them. After a time, you begin to feel thin and not all here. Your energy is scattered. Bring it back to your body. Call all of yourselves back to you.

When I call all my selves back to me, where is *back to me*? I can choose where that is. Is it here or over there? If I see *over there* as sitting on the roof of my garage, then do I call myself back to that place as a choice? I am the observer looking at both choices. I choose the new place—that is me sitting on the roof of the garage—looking down at me who is looking up at me. When I pull the self back to me from that new location, that becomes *teleportation*. Teleportation is a matter of bilocation until you pull one of yourselves to a new place and choose that perspective. From the new perspective, it is teleportation.

Then I bilocate again and pull myself—my perception of myself—back to sitting in the chair in my gazebo, the place where I started my journey.

What Matters

Understanding doesn't matter. We can't really understand. Mattering doesn't matter. We make matter, matter. That's so funny. Mattering matter. I play in the realm of energy. Matter is a byproduct of energy slowing down and contracting. Rikka Zimmerman says that space is what is important. She believes that space is more important than energy and she gives even energy the limiting conditions of matter. I would say that none of it matters. The Universe is just a huge playground; a sand box we can play in and experience. How we do that is up to us. How would it feel if we all wanted Peace? We could do that. And it would be very peaceful, until it wasn't. Someone would get bored and break the silence of Peace. This is a multi-faceted and multi-dimensional world. We co-created it. And the world starts with the energy existing in space. We add time and then we have experiences.

This morning I played with time. Moving it forward and backward. I thought that I would end at my death if I moved too far forward. But I could still see what was happening beyond my life. So, my awareness does not die. The energy of us—or our spirit or our energy body, whatever you want to call it—does not lose its awareness.

Dreamtime

Dreamtime is an experience when we are awake, the same as conscious dreaming or lucid dreaming when you are awake.

They are also the same as Shamanic Journeys in many traditions. It doesn't matter what we call it. It only matters that we do it. One way to do it is to name it or to say we are doing it. It is more powerful if we say it out loud.

When we name our intention, we bring it into being. We don't have to master a skill. We just need to yield to our higher self and get out of the way. We are really getting out of the way of ourselves. Give yourself an invitation to shift your perspective. When you shift your perspective, you are stepping into another dimension.

Dreamtime happens in space. The space between all worlds. All you have to do is be willing to step into that space.

You also have to be willing to play like a child. In my prayer this morning, I asked to become the energy of a child who is pleased and looks at the world with wonder. I said, *God, make me the energy of a child who is pleased with the world and looks at it with wonder. Also make me as wise as the oldest sage.* I required both the wisdom of the sage and the wonder of a child.

Imagination opens our door to perceiving. We need to give up our need to know and our understanding. We endlessly pursue knowledge to feel safe and in control. Then knowledge takes control. Our obsession to define and interpret what we see keeps us from seeing what is in front of us. Getting out of the box of knowledge is stepping into awareness, dreamtime, and imagination.

Patterns Limit Us

We are habituated by our patterns.

> *I sing my power song several times through, repeating it until the melody is ingrained in me and the audience. Then I break my*

pattern. As I share it with a group for a final time, I don't sing the last note. And there is a silence as everyone waits for the completion. But completion doesn't come. I think about those who suffer from OCD. They must be going crazy from something left undone.

There are those who need to finish projects before they can go on to the next one. There are also those who rarely finish anything. Our patterns habituate us. They control us through their habituation. Sometimes this is good. We have good healthy habits that keep us on a healthy path. But it is still control. Change your perception and you let go of the pattern of control and step into the freedom of … what? Whatever you choose. Whatever you put your attention and focus on.

Without the control of habit, we have more freedom. Some would say that we are more spacious. To maintain the pattern is actually a lot of work. It takes a great deal of work to maintain a pattern or the story of why you are the way you are. *I've always done this. My mother did this.* And then life steps in to support and acknowledge that story. That is a lot of work and energy to maintain that pattern. It is much easier to be free.

We can obtain our gifts and our freedom by simply claiming them. When others see them in us, it is easier to recognize them in ourselves. When others recognize them in us and share what they have recognized with us, we can sometimes see our gifts and our freedom more easily. Or we sometimes reject them out of hand, by saying, *Oh no. I'm not really that good* (or beautiful or talented or whatever). But it isn't necessary to recognize ourselves through others. Our gifts and our freedom are already inside us; we are simply removing the barrier to recognizing them. The barrier is the limiting pattern. Let go of any limiting patterns and change your perception.

Sacred Technologies for Dancing and Seeing Energy

- **Bilocation.** Split your perception into two and see yourself in another place, such as another room or on a chair across from where you are. If you believe you can't split your perception, then pretend or imagine you can. Perceive the world from this new location. What does it look like? Then turn to face your original self. When you have changed your perception call all yourselves back to you. Say, *I now call all of my selves back to me, clean, clear, and abundant.*
- **Entrain your energy** to a higher energy like Peace, Love, or Joy. Feel what those energies feel like. You can name energy whatever you like. How do you entrain your energy to it? By asking the Universe to show you Joy and then by stepping into that Joy and hanging out there. You are simultaneously naming it and claiming it.
- **Listen to silence.** Look for the silence between the sounds of the birds, frogs, and crickets. Listen to the silence when the wind stops. Breathe in that silence. This will silence your mind and put you into spaciousness.
- **Lucid dreaming.** When you go to sleep tonight, ask to have a lucid dream. In that lucid dream, look for your hands or your feet or some object. Relate to that object. Know that you are dreaming. Have an intention to do something in your dream. Once you realize you are dreaming, then do that thing you intended to do. You can also ask to learn something. Once you realize you are dreaming, then ask to learn about what you want to learn.

- **Dreamtime.** You can also do lucid dreaming while you are awake. Imagine that you are dreaming while you are awake. And then you are. Now ask what you want to see. And then you will. You must be totally relaxed to do this.

 Low vibrational thoughts are the junk foods of the mind.

Energy and Food

The state of our thoughts is intimately connected to the vibrational frequency of our health and the food we ingest. So much has been written about food that I don't wish to add to the plethora of divergent and misinformation as well as to the helpful yet overwhelming information out there. I believe the most important thing about food is what we *believe to be true* about it. If you believe being a vegetarian is the best way, then be that. If you are a meat eater and believe you need your protein, then be that.

The power of your belief is more important than the content of your belief. Our thought directs the reality of our

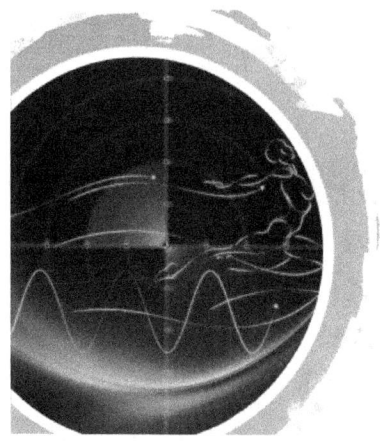

Energy Frequencies

Healthy Body (daytime)	62-72 MHZ
During Illness (infection)	52-58 MHZ
During Cancer	40-42 MHZ
Near Death	24-26 MHZ

world. Many highly evolved masters need very little food. And I do believe we eat way too much. I also believe we should enjoy and be grateful for what we do eat. A healthy body has a naturally high vibrational frequency. See the chart below.

The Vibrational Frequency of our health (from The Health Laboratory at www.healthlaboratorylive.com. See Resources).

We can intentionally shift the vibration of a situation or of ourselves to an elevated state of clarity and empowerment. We can do this through the food we eat, our physical exercise, our mental state, our emotional state, and our spiritual connection. I would also call this a mind body spirit alignment, the process of Joyfinity. How does this work?

So! The energy of your body is dependent on the vibrational frequency of your physical cells, which is in-turn dependent on the food you eat plus other factors such as your state of health (both physical and emotional).

Food, when digested, becomes energy that is then transferred to our body and cells via a process known as *biological transmutation*. The longer the time between when it is harvested and when we eat it, the lower its frequency generally becomes. (Note: bananas are one of the few, if not the only, fruits that increases in electromagnetic energy if picked unripe; www.healthlaboratorylive.com.)

Foods and herbs with the highest energetic frequency include these:

- Fresh, organic fruits and vegetables
- Green smoothies
- Fresh, whole herbs
- Superfoods such as fresh blueberries and spirulina

100 percent pure, therapeutic grade essential oils are nourishing:
Being hydrated is also essential because water is required for electrical conductivity. Water can actually store and deliver energy.

> "Essential oils are whole concentrates, containing volatile aroma compounds from plants. Clinical studies have shown that therapeutic grade essential oils have the highest frequency of any natural substance known to man! With rose essential oil having the highest recorded frequency at 320 MHz" (The Health Laboratory).

This is good news to me because I love roses and rose oil! So the food we eat and our attitude about that food affect our vibrational frequencies. Because thought affects our frequencies and words come from those thoughts, the energy of language also affects our frequency.

Language as Energy

AUM

Today I noticed that the use of *Um* when people are starting to speak is a little like *AUM*. The sounds are similar but not exactly the same. Also I noticed that the *ah* that gets expressed in an exhale when we let go of something is also like the *A* in *AUM*. Is this the natural order of God expressing its energy through us to aid us in our deliberations? I think it is.

The *A* sound is the same as the sound of God enclosed by the consonants gee and dee. *Ah* is the expression of God energy going out externally and eternally, while the gee and dee form the materiality of matter and bring an essence into being in the present moment. In *AUM* the *A* expresses God and the *U* sound sends it out while beginning to close it down into form. And the *M* brings it home, into ourselves. The energy flows back into each of us as individuals. AUM is a completely circuitous expression of God energy.

In my habitual pattern of words, I have two *go-to* words: *So* and *okay*. So, how do they fit in? *So* is the first part of *So hum*, a popular mantra that is also called *So ham*. The more western way of expressing *AUM* is *OM*. Or a very new age way is *Home*. I think of these as the microwave version of meditating with sound. It's fast cooking on high heat. Sometimes it's good and sometimes we need to use a slow cooker like a crock pot. There is no right or wrong way to express the I AM. And that isn't even that close to AUM! Language has vibration and vibration either raises us up or it slows us down. We can be conscious in what we are saying.

Bellows Breath to Hummingbird Wings

When I finish my morning meditation, I generally include an *Ahmen*. Then I sing the Ahmen up and down my chakras until I get to my brain chakra and then I sing a high *e* sound that rattles my teeth. I throw in a low didgeridoo sound, whoaah, to vibrate the lowest chakras even more.

I follow this sound vibration with a bellows breath on each chakra individually and then raise the vibration higher and higher by individually quickening each chakra and ending with a hummingbird flutter in each chakra. I then do a bellows breath and raise the vibration of each and all chakras together and end with a hummingbird vibration on all chakras together, including the ones above and below my head and feet.

Then I do a roll up the front of my body through the chakras. I call this rolling sadness into Joy. Followed by a roll up the back and up each of the sides and then the whole body rolling up together. A huge rush of energy pours in from the top when I am done.

Healing

I wait. And I ask, *Now what?* I notice that my face feels weird. It almost hurts. I move it all around as though for the Lion Pose in yoga. It still feels *not right*. I decide that I have moved the energy out through my crown and face but that some of it has gotten stuck. So, I repeat the bellows-to-hummingbird exercise with my mind. And I breathe the energy out and in through my head. Then I notice that my neck is weird on the left side. I think that some of the energy got stuck there also. So, I breathe the energy through that place. I do this twice and then decide I might as well also breathe through my right shoulder, which has been giving me trouble. Then I bellows-to-hummingbird my breath in my shoulder.

As I write this, all distractions in my head, face, neck, and shoulder are gone. I ask what my path is and wait. Now what. I ask for rose petals and the smell of roses so that I may find my way. I think of the smell of roses and am reminded of Gandalf being lost in the mines of Moria and finding his way using his nose. I think that my nose is also good when I can't see the path. And then I think that a light shining on my path would also be helpful. To make certain that I don't get lost. I ask for a light to show me the way.

Try placing fireworks in each of your chakras.

Fire Works

This morning I played with placing fireworks in each of my chakras. I start at the bottom and open the root chakra and place in it a brilliant display of fireworks. It can be mostly reds here. But I like also my favorite fireworks, which are the gold sparkles that trail down in long tails.

Then I move up to the second chakra, where orange dominates. I open this chakra and see the fireworks happening in my belly. Then I move to the power chakra and see the fireworks of the central sun, which are the yellow and gold of the sun. Next, it's the heart chakra and the pink and green colors erupt into the sky and I am amazed. And that sky is contained in my heart.

I open my throat and see the blue and silver sparkles of the fireworks in my throat and I open it to the heaven that resides within it. My brain is alight with all the colors and white predominates. There is also a deep blue. The cave inside my brain has fireworks exploding on the roof of the cave and I sit below to look up at the ceiling, which has risen so far that the sky is contained within it. Then I go up to my crown where lavender pearls and sparkles rise up into the sky and there is no end to the heights that they reach. But still all are contained within my being.

Then I decide to explode all the fireworks at once from all my chakras in a kind of grand finale with the *boom, boom, boom,* everywhere all at once. And then I think, *What if I take the boom, boom finale into each of my chakras and start over.* I do. *And what will the finale be then?* I don't know. But there is only quiet.

What If It Is All Just a DANCE

We dance with our thoughts. We dance with our words and the sounds we make. We dance with love and our relationships. We dance with power. *Will I or won't I create, or do, this?* We dance with our wisdom. What kind of dance do we have with wisdom? I'll try this path. No, I'll try that path. We dance with each chakra, seeing the energy of each one flowing back and forth, giving and taking, and we also dance up through the entire channel energy system. Two energetic elevators passing in the night, dancing and reaching out to each other in a subtle tango. I am reminded of the "Hernando's Hideaway" tango song.

How do we dance with our thoughts? We play with *I am this.* Fill in the blank. I am a teacher. *A teacher of what?* the other asks. I suggest, *Of spirit,* and the other says, *No, you are a teacher of architecture and science.* There is no difference, I say, and the dance begins.

We dance in the throat chakra. *But what will you manifest?* the other asks. And the dance begins. I reach out toward the other and I say, *I will write a book.*

But what can you write about? he asks.

Whatever comes into my mind, I reply.

But will it be useful to me?

Maybe or maybe not, but it will be useful to me, I reply.

But it must be useful to me also, the other says.

I respond. *If it is authentic to me then it is useful to all because we are connected.*

Then I move down to my heart. I expand out as much as I can. I seem to think this is the most important chakra because I know that Love transforms all energies. And then the dance continues. *And what do you want to transform?* my dance partner asks.

All lower energies, I answer.

But what are those energies? And why do you call them lower?

I mean no disrespect by calling them lower. They are simply more contracted and vibrate more slowly. Anger and fear. I know they have a use. I know that if they are present, then I must feel them. And now the dance is in full swing. We tango. Fear and love, and hate and love, and then there is no dance partner anymore. The direction of the attention of Love dissolves all else. And now, *Where am I with no partner to dance with?*

So, I move down into the power chakra. I dance with power. Long ago I gave up *power over* and began to dance with the *power of*. But power of what? The power of Love and the power of Joy and the power of Gratitude. The power of Beauty and the power of Divine Perfection. These are all wonderful powers to dance with and so I do. Each of the energies receives more power and we dance. Approach and retreat. Approach and retreat. It is the tango.

And then I ask, *But what is the purpose?* and I move on to the second chakra, the sacral chakra of wisdom. *Why do I dance with Joy?* I ask. *Because I am Joy and I dance for the joy of dancing. I am peace and I dance for the peace of being peace.* I am here to be. *Be what?* To be Peace and Joy and Magic. I am that I am.

Then the dance has finished. The music has stopped playing. But I remember. And I hold the memory of the dance within me, and I am that. If I should forget for a moment, I can simply recall the dance. Recall the music. And the dance will begin again.

If you should want to do this dance for yourself. First start with the mind and the third eye chakra. If you can bring the energy of your mind along, the rest will go smoothly.

We all need to store, increase, and flow our energy. We can do this by obeying the rules of energy. Let go of our limiting patterns. Eat well and believe in our choices. Dance and play with energy. Then we can learn to define and refine the energies around us.

 Blossoming and growing is authentic.

CHAPTER 8

Allow WOW: Energy of Joyfinity

 I don't have to bring in Joy. Just stop repressing it.

Joyfinity System of Energetics

Acceptance to gratitude to Joy

Inspire and infuse energy into our physical body

Choose our path; our path chooses us

Commit to our path absolutely

Play

A Pivotal Joy Experience

> *The sunrise over the Bimini Flats at the marina is spectacular. It would be impossible not to feel the magnificence. Fingers of pink, lavender, and gold touch the aqua sea. I am in such gratitude. I am thankful for being alive and for each breath of air. For the retreat I am attending. For the couch I sit on. For the sparkling water and the sunrise. I then ask God, "Show me how much Joy I can possibly be." How much Joy can God be through me? I wait. And then I am showered with a billion sparkles of light. I feel my body explode out into the universe as billions of sparkles of Joy. I wonder. Will I come back together again? Or will I remain a billion pieces of light out in the universe. I come back together. But then I wonder. Can I walk? I can walk and as I walk I hear the grass giggling under my feet.*

This was my experience as I was greeting the morning sunrise on February 15, 2016, in the Bahamas at Bimini, and saying my Morning Prayer. At that time there were only Peace, Love, and Joy in my list of the aspects of God. The others were added later. After learning that I could indeed walk, I then wondered if I could eat and swallow food. I went into the buffet at the hotel, and the food tasted exquisite. Even the water was exquisite. I ran up to people and said that I was so full of Joy that I couldn't contain it. They said, "Don't contain it." So, I didn't. I shared it. And I am still sharing it today. I can relive that experience any time I choose, although it is different each time. It is different because I am different. I can simply go there and feel the exquisite Joy of the billion sparkles of light that I am.

Joyfinity: Acceptance, Gratitude, and Celebration

The expressions of Love and pure Joy emit the highest resonance of all energies, while laughter broadcasts the lightest of our emotional frequencies, according to the Health Laboratory (healthlaboratorylive.com). I use the term *Joyfinity* to name an energy that is high, pure, and infinite. It is infinite in its magnitude and it is eternal. At its highest level, or frequency, Joy can contain all other frequencies as does Love. But Joy starts out at a slightly lower frequency than Love. When we are truly joyful at its highest frequency, which is also its purest form, we are on an ever-increasing energetic path to the center of the wheel. At the center, there is no difference in the energies. They are unified at the center of Source. Just as when we are absolutely peaceful, there is no difference at the center of everything. This is why I use the wheel with its spokes of Joy, Peace, Gratitude, and all the other aspects as paths home to ourselves. Home is at the center where Love as the universal Source resides.

Joy, Glory, and Love all contain celebration. At the very highest frequency, there is no difference. But remember that it starts with acceptance.

Acceptance and Allowance

What is it that we need to accept? Anything that we resist. It might be pain, lack, or poverty; or too much wealth or poor health or too old an age or too young an age. We tend to resist any condition we have placed on ourselves. Even if we believe that someone else has placed the condition on us. What are the conditions? That our parents were such and such or we grew up in a certain way? When we accept the conditions, then what? We move forward. Acceptance is the first step in moving forward. Acceptance and allowance are slightly different. Acceptance is *Okay, I acknowledge that it is there. I won't continue to deny it.* Allowance is *I know that it is there, and I am okay with it being* there. I will let go of resisting it and I will allow it to be there.

Gratitude

The next step is giving gratitude for what is. After we have allowed and accepted some event, we are ready to give thanks for what has occurred. We are ready to be grateful for the parents we had. We can finally see that there is a silver lining. That if the event hadn't occurred, we never would have … Fill in the blank. We would not have learned of our power to do things we had never done before. We learn many life lessons through a loss or a negative occurrence. It is these lessons we are grateful for. We are not grateful for the loss itself. Or for whatever the negative occurrence is. We are grateful for the life lessons and the opportunities the lesson brings.

Gratitude is the middle state of change. Gratitude is sending an energy out into the Universe. It is saying thank you for what has occurred. It is letting the Universe know that we are at peace and maybe even a little happy about what we have experienced as a result of an event. Because we are giving thanks to the Universe, it responds to us. And we begin to feel joyful. Gratitude is the catalyst that sends our positive and high vibrating energy out. It returns to us fourfold. And then we experience Joy. And the celebration begins.

Celebration

The final step is celebrating what is. By the time we get to celebrating, we might notice that the condition no longer exists. Either it never did, or it has transformed. Celebration comes from the energy of Love. And Love transforms all things into higher energy forms.

Or we celebrate the life we had with the person we lost. Or we celebrate the lesson we learned from the event that occurred. The more gratitude we feel the more Joy is returned to us. When we share that Joy, we radiate it out to the universe and those around us. Then the Universe celebrates with us. When we are filled with Love, we often find that the event we thought occurred never did. Or our pain is gone or the event that happened wasn't really negative at all. It was just an event. An experience.

There are many ways we can celebrate. Food and drink are often accompaniments. So are talking with friends and laughing. Laughter is one way to punctuate that celebration.

Laughing the Chakras

We can laugh to celebrate, and we can also laugh to integrate the celebration into the body. I've written about laughter many times and its many physical and mental benefits, such as the endorphins and lowered blood pressure that we get when we laugh. I have also noticed that the contraction that happens with a good belly laugh is similar to the contraction that happens when we do the technique of *rolling sadness into joy*. I wondered what would happen if I tried this same laughing contraction in each of my chakras. I was totally delighted. I got a similar experience to thrumming but with a sound. The sound of laughter. The sound of laughter has a definite positive influence. I love this technique. It gives a positive vibration to your entire body. And it is fun! So try this technique.

Sacred Technology: Laughing the Chakras

- **Laugh in each of your chakras.** How do you do that? When you do a deep belly laugh, go down to the first chakra, the chakra of safety. Think of a horse whinnying and a chortle. This laugh is very low and slow.

- **Then do a belly laugh.** It doesn't have to be about anything. Just start laughing. Notice that your first two chakras have strong contractions when you belly laugh. Simply notice the contractions.

- **Then see if you can bring** that same laughing contraction one chakra higher into your power chakra. It is a very tight contraction but somewhat lighter than the one in the belly.

- **Now move the laughing contraction** up to your heart chakra. It is lighter yet. Think of the sound of *Ahh*. Turn *Ahh* into a laugh. Think of a monk laughing.

- **Next go to your throat chakra.** This contraction may feel more like a chuckle. If you are not chuckling, then pretend that you are or start chuckling. It is a little like the ringing of bells.

- **Go to the third eye chakra.** This will be a light giggle. The bells will tinkle as though they are fairy bells. It is a high-pitched giggling. Think of *Eee*.

- **Now go to the crown chakra.** The sound of laughing this high is so refined it is a chortle with a hum. Because of its refined nature, it seems to gather energy from the first chakra. It is gentler. It is refined and gentle at the same time. Just think of *mmm.*
- **Now go back** and give yourself a good belly laugh. What is that like?

Jellyfish Breathing

This morning's breathing exercise and prayer led to a tree moving at least two feet closer to me. Let me explain.

First, I ran through at least two complete sets of channel breaths and activated each chakra. Then I breathed each chakra working my way up.

I asked about abundance and thought my solar plexus and throat chakra were blocking the abundance energy from coming through me and out into the world. Certainly, my throat has had issues with my thyroid, not speaking and over speaking. I have always surrounded myself with people who speak too much. And when I am away from them, I tend to speak too much. Finding the right balance is the key, I told myself. So I did the breath of fire on my throat chakra. I looked around. The maple tree in front of me, which is on the other side of the deck, seemed to jump two feet forward. I know in my rational mind that it didn't, but all of a sudden, I could almost reach out and touch it. When had it moved so close to me? I was so grateful for its presence that I wept with Joy.

Then I did a few more fire breaths on my third eye chakra and did more solar plexus breathing. I have to place my hands above and below the solar plexus to know that I am doing it correctly and not activating the chakras above and below it. I am now beginning to feel it without the use of my hands.

On the first go around after doing some straw breaths (see Dr. Sue Morter's book, *The Energy Codes*), the energy coming through feels soft. The second time through, when the energy came in from above, it floated down in waves like a jellyfish waving or breathing its tentacles as it slowly descended down through all parts of me.

I was reminded of an experience I had many years ago while doing conscious breathing and I was surrounded by hundreds of jellyfish all over my body while they breathed me. Now I see that it is just energy and that it is the motion of the jellyfish that is happening. No jellyfish, just energy like jellyfish in motion. My mind makes that moving energy into jellyfish to explain the presence of the unique motion. That's okay. I like it. But I know that it is just energy floating and undulating down in a certain rhythm of breath. In this instance that rhythm was the same rhythm as the rhythm of the Universe.

Sacred Technologies: Activation of the Jellyfish Energy.

- **Jellyfish.** Inhale into your lower abdomen and then exhale down into the earth as far as you can go. Breathe into your belly from as high as you can reach into the heaven and then breathe out into the earth as far as you can go. Repeat by breathing up from the earth and releasing the breath into the heavens. Feel each breath and flip the direction of the breath at the belly. Feel the air as it carries the energy of spirit. Repeat until you feel waves of energy, like a jellyfish breathing your body.

- **Universe breathing.** Place your hands beside your ears about a foot away. Face the palms in. Wait and listen and feel. You will feel a pulsing in your hands. This pulsing is the wave energy of the universe. It is the same rhythm of the Universe breathing.

The Roll of Enlivening

Rolling Sadness into Joy.

For many years I have practiced what I call *Rolling Sadness into Joy*. I describe this in the first chapter. There are also descriptions and a video of that practice on my website (www.triciajeanecroyle.com).

What I am doing is pulling some contractive energy up into some expansive energy and then letting the expansive energy fall into it. What this does is harmonize the expansion with the contraction of each of the energies as they mix and transform. This was and still remains good practice.

The Roll of Enlivening

The Rolling Sadness into Joy exercise has evolved. As has my understanding of how it works. Now I roll the contraction from the root chakra to my crown. I also roll it from the chakra in the earth to the chakra in the heavens.

I roll it all the way up, contracting each area of each chakra and in between each chakra as I go. I am exhaling as I do this. Then as I reach the top, I sigh and exhale as I let it go and then the air rushes in through my crown and down, washing my entire system.

My new practice is to simply roll the energy without labeling it. We don't have to name the energy to transform it. Mixing contractive energy like anger with expansive energy like Peace harmonizes the energy. Master your energy, master your life.

I feel a gasp or a longing in some part of my body. A gasp in the second chakra or a burning in my nose that is reminiscent of sadness. Then I start the process. There was a longing on my back of being left out of the process and forgotten. And then my sides felt that they had been left out.

This morning as I did this exercise, I decided my back side was not being engaged in the process enough. So, I reversed the process and starting at the tailbone I rolled my back in an arch stretching up to my crown. I tilted my head back and let the energy go out my forehead and top of my crown.

Then my sides felt left out, and I started squeezing them in at the base and rolled that squeeze on both sides together up to my head. But I got stuck there and had to roll through my head separately on the back and sides. The result. I was totally enlivened! This was my own personal yoga practice.

Yes, I was rolling any sadness or any other contractive emotion that I wished to transform into Joy. But I didn't have to name the energy that was transforming. I was just rolling my grounding energy up through my expansive energy. The release at the top allowed the energy of spirit to come rushing in.

I've tried rolling down from up above. It doesn't seem necessary as the energy rushes in all by itself. What shall I call this process? The enlivening roll. *The Roll of Enlivening.*

Joyfinity System of Energetics

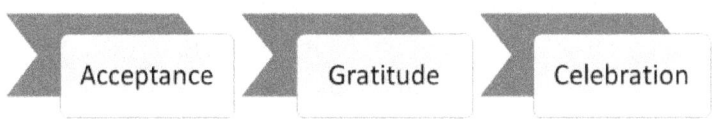

The Energy of Joyfinity

The energy of Joyfinity is the energy of Joy in its purest form. It is the energy of Joy meeting the infinite. It can be approached by practicing acceptance, gratitude, and celebration during all of our life's experiences. And by practicing the exercises found throughout this book like *laughing your chakras* and *Universe breathing*. When we add the enlivening practices with the breathing practices, we can infuse the energy into every cells of our body. The clarity that this provides enables us to see and walk our paths in Joy. A Joy that is both infinite and eternal.

When we master our energy, we master our life. These practices are simply a beginning of that mastery. When we are the WOW of all parts combined in the unity of one; and the POW of our power is light and not forced; when we VOW to live life as God's expression of Love; when we let go of HOW and become our perception; when we are willing to experience all energies, both expansive and contractive; when we are present for undefined and pure energy, then acceptance, gratitude, and celebration turn into WOW. Then we have mastered our energy and our life. This is the WOW of energy mastery.

May God give you
For every storm, a rainbow,
For every tear, a smile,
For every care, a promise,
And a blessing in each trial.
For every problem life sends,
A faithful friend to share,
For every sigh, a sweet song,
And an answer for each prayer.

—Old Irish Blessing

CHAPTER 9

The WOW:
of Sacred Technologies

 The solution isn't fighting back. Open up your heart and bring consciousness to the table.

Sacred Technologies: Tools for letting go of beliefs and stories and transforming emotions and feelings into higher energy frequencies

Rolling sadness into Joy

Eat with the awareness of Source

Infuse Love into power.

Anchor with sound

Create fireworks in your chakras.

Swim your energy

Laughter: laugh your chakras.

The sacred technologies are gathered in the back of the book here so that they are easier to access. If you want more detail as to how they affected me or an explanation as to why you are doing them, go back to the chapter in the book. The descriptions are not exactly the same. Sometimes I have changed the details so as to clarify how to do them. These descriptions tend to be shorter.

Chapter 1 Sacred Technologies: The WOW of Energy Mastery

1. **Increase Receiving**. Say *I now choose to receive …* (Love, health or wealth). Say whatever you would like to receive. Say it three times. You could also say, *I choose to receive receiving.*
2. **Embody Receiving**. Breathe in slowly and out slowly as you count to seven. Do this seven times. Feel the energy of embodying receiving as you inhale and feel the letting go as you exhale and create room for more receiving.
3. **Swim Your Energy with Breaststroke.** Do the breaststroke with your energy when you are not in the water. See it move as you pull your arms down to your side. When the tips of your fingers meet. Roll the backs of your hands together in a kind of reverse praying position. Then raise them up over your head and turn them out. See your energy moving as you do this. Add your breath to the exercise. Breathe in as you pull your arms down and exhale out as you push the energy up and out through your crown chakra. You

can make this as big as you like, dropping the energy way below your feet and way above your head. Do at least forty energy breaststrokes. This will get the channeled energy moving smoothly. Your energy is already doing this, and you are just consciously participating in moving it along. Adding this movement with your conscious breathing will assist you in embodying source energy.

4. **Swim the Breaststroke and Add Your Conscious Energy.** Swim the breaststroke with conscious breathing and mantra energy when you are in the water. This will get the energy moving smoothly along the core of your being. Adding your conscious breathing with this movement will assist you in embodying source energy. Adding a mantra will bring your mind along into the exercise. Add the mantra, *I am open to receiving energy.* Time this mantra with the rhythm of your breaststroke.

5. **Return Your Energy.** Pull your energy back to yourself consciously. Say *I now bring all my energy back to me, clean, clear, and abundant.* Say this three times.

6. **Roll Sadness into Joy.** Think of something sad. Feel where the sadness is located in your body. Is there a contraction or a burning somewhere? Contract or lift the sadness up to your heart chakra. Let it drop back down. Roll it up to your throat. How does it feel there? Let it go back down. Roll it up to your third eye. How does it feel there? Let it fall back down. Roll it up to your crown chakra. How does it feel there? Let it go

back down. You can also flow the energy in the other direction with simple noticing.

7. **Notice the Rolling.** Notice your crown chakra and then notice your sacral chakra. Notice wherever you are holding sadness. Then allow the energy from your crown chakra to flow down into the sacral chakra. This is not a physical contraction of the body. It is simply the noticing of your energy. How does that feel? Repeat noticing the energy dropping down from the heart, the throat, and the third eye chakras.

8. **Tickle the Earth.** Feel into the earth with the energy of your feet. Tickle the center of the earth. Take a deep breath. Do this three times.

9. **Move Energy in a Triangle.** Open your palms and see the sun above your head, your mind in your right palm, and your spirit in your left palm. Circulate the energy around the triangle. See it as a white ball moving from apex to apex. And then see it as a continuously moving stream of light. Then change directions.

10. **Breathe like a Slinky**. See your hands held out with a slinky in them. This is a kind of toy where you can raise your hands up and down one at a time, and the slinky will fall to one side or the other. Now imagine that you have an energetic slinky the colors of the rainbow. Play with that rainbow raising one hand up and down and then the other so that the rainbow flows back and forth into the opposite hand. Inhale and exhale as you do this. Now feel the energy flowing up and down

your body as you play with your slinky. Continue until you have the energy in your body moving.

11. **Identify Energy Using Your Senses.** Imagine you are holding a lemon. Feel, smell, and taste lemon. What kind of energy is it? When you begin to salivate, know that you are embodying the energy of lemon.

Chapter 2 Sacred Technologies: The WOW Energy of Unity

12. **Being Happy with Being Alone**

    Ask yourself, *What do I fear in being alone?*

    Ask yourself, *What is it that I don't want to know about myself?*

    Then forgive yourself for whatever it is. Say, *I forgive myself for …*

    Say, *I am okay with being alone.*

    Say, *I even like being alone.*

    Say, *I cherish this time that I have to be alone.*

    Ask, *Who am I?*

13. **Vanilla Ice Cream.** Eat ice cream or any other fun food with the intent of having fun. Eat it slowly with the intent of having pleasure. Allow it to melt and meld with your body. Ask God what the ice cream tastes like. How does it feel as it goes down? Listen to what Source has to tell you about this. Know that it nourishes your body at the same time that it is fun to eat.

14. **Open Doors Inward.** Pull your awareness back against your spine. Look forward. See a door. Go toward

the door and open it inward, toward you. Turn around facing back to where you were and see yourself. Turn around and look forward. Step back against your spine. See another door. Open the door inward. Turn around and see yourself standing there looking out. Turn forward and look out. See another door. Open it inward. Turn around and face yourself. Then turn forward and look out. See another door. Repeat ten times.

15. **The Glow Stick.** Imagine you have a glow stick that runs from your crown chakra to your root chakra. It is glowing. Tiny gold tendrils run out of the ends and from the sides of the glow stick. Tendrils also run out of all our chakras that connect into the universal matrix. Send out information, about your thoughts and desires through these very fine golden lines. Wait and see and listen. What did you receive back?

16. **Joining Energies**. Say three times: *I accept the light of God. We are one. Our lights are so bright that they overlap and we have joined. We are one.*

Chapter 3 Sacred Technologies: The WOW Energy of Power

17. **Integrating Love and Power.** See yourself standing on the top of a mountain at the top of the world. You look down and admire all that you have created. You are, after all, on the top of the world. Soften this feeling with love and cherish all that you see below you. Feel the softness that love brings without any relinquishing of power.

18. **Integrate Lightness into Energy and Power**. Roll the sadness into Joy without the contraction. Roll sadness into joy by physically contracting your body and rolling the contraction upward. Then let it drop back down. Do this three times. Then roll the energy of sadness without the contraction from a lower chakra where you have stored it up into a higher chakra such as your heart or third eye chakra. Roll your sadness up into joy. And then let it drop back down bringing the Joy down into where the sadness was held. Do this three times. Then do it with the simple motion of your fingers. Do it outside yourself with your fingers and notice the energy flow. See how small you can make the movement.

19. **Raise the Energy of Power.** Contract your energy in and expand out as large and as small as you can. Do this three times. Then move your fingers as if you were expanding in and out. Do this three times. The more slowly and with focus you can do this, the more powerfully your energy will be raised. It is the same energy as a bellows on a fire. Notice with your observer witness that you are doing this.

Chapter 4 Sacred Technologies: The WOW Energy of God Principle

20. **Enlivening Meditation Using the Chalice Vision**. Use the vision I had about a chalice in chapter 4 as a meditation. Read it out loud to yourself or record it. Visualize each sentence as you go.

21. **United.** Repeat three times: *You are God. I am God. You are God. I am God. You are God. I am God. We are God. We are one. United together in thought, word, and action.*

22. **Deep Dive in a Bubble.** Go deep down into your being by descending in a bubble as if it were a submarine going deep into the ocean. Watch as tiny bubbles drift up from your bubble. Watch yourself descend. Look for the quiet-of-God contact. Know that it comes from the silence within and go deeper. Let no thought that is not Love come through you. Bad does not enter here. This is why you have entered the depth of yourself, to contact God. This is how the body returns to the spirit that made it and how it resides in that energy.

23. **Swim Your Energy.** Do the breaststroke with your energy. See it move as you pull your arms down to your side. When the tips of your fingers meet. Roll the backs of your hands together in a kind of reverse praying action. Then raise them up over your head and turn them out. See your energy moving as you do this. Add your breath to the exercise. Breathe in as you pull your arms down and exhale out as you push the energy up and out through your crown chakra. You can also do this when you are actually swimming.

24. **Channel Breath as You Walk.** Do the channel breath when you go for a walk or a run. Inhale each breath as you step on your right foot and exhale each breath as you step on your left foot. And then switch, by bringing the energy up your left foot and out your

right foot. If this is too quick, then do it every third or fourth step. Experiment with your own natural stepping and breathing rhythms. Run the energy from your crown into the earth and from the earth into your crown. Be the energy as you do this.

25. **Hummingbird Wings.** Ask that each chakra double its vibration rate. And then again by two and again by two and again by two. Do this until your chakras are vibrating as fast as hummingbird wings and then times two. Then ask that all chakras radiate together and they then also increase by two and by two .

26. **Thrumming.** Add sound to the vibrating of your chakras going at hummingbird wing speed. Vibrate your lips by putting your top teeth on your bottom lip and making a humming sound. Run through all your chakras independently and then together.

Chapter 5 How to WOW: Energy of Manifestation

27. **Experience Embodiment.** Sit your awareness in the lower three chakras. Breathe in and out from a place in each of the three lower chakras. See a ball of light expanding and contracting with your breath, in and out three times in each chakra. Contract the root chakra up into the pelvic bowl and breathe in and out from the second chakra. Contract in as far as you can and then breathe out as far as you can from chakras two and three. Then let out a sigh, making it audible. This will integrate that energy into your physical body.

28. **Experience More Magic.** Say three times, *I choose to see the magic that already exists in the world.* Say three times, *I am grateful for the magic that already exists in the world.*
29. **Let Go of the Need for Approval.** Let go of the need for anything. Allow it to be okay if you get approval or you don't get approval. Approve of yourself for letting go of the need for approval. You can fill in the blank with any need you have.
30. **Then Let Go of the Need for Need**. How? Just say, *I now let go of the need for needing.* Say this three times.
31. **See Peace.** Ask God to show you what peace feels, looks, and tastes like. Listen. Experience. Then go about your day and ask, *Where is the peace in that? What does peace look like here?* Watch as you become more peaceful. What happens around you?

Chapter 6 Here and WOW: Energy of Transmuting

32. **Inside Outside.** Look at something or someone outside yourself. Now pull your awareness inside yourself. Look outside. Now inside. Go back and forth increasing the speed until there is no difference between outside and inside. And you are one with the outside and inside.
33. **Be the Peace You Want to See in the World**. Call up the energy of Peace. Infuse it into every cell of your body. Breathe peace in and out. Breath peace into all your chakras one at a time. Breathe peace out through your heart chakra to the world. Stand in that place throughout your day.

34. **Peace at Bedtime**. Ask yourself, *How did my day change because I was Peace. What did I notice?*
35. **Interacting with Clouds.** Watch the clouds as they pass overhead. See what shapes appear. Are you creating them or are they already there and you are simply noticing and recognizing what is there?
36. **Bubbles of Color.** Imagine that you have a giant bubble wand and are pulling a huge bubble up from your feet over and through your entire body. Run through all the colors of the rainbow.
37. **Let Go of Scary Dreams.** Bring into the light any scary or struggling dreams you have had by remembering them. Then let them go. Then you won't have to repeat them.

Chapter 7 Now to WOW: Purity of Energy

38. **Perception of the Portals of Allow and Notice.** Take a deep breath and exhale. Just look around. Forget about it all. When you look around, eventually, the portals will show up. And then say, *Oh, there you are.* Say, *Thank you* and let it be. When they disappear, don't try to hang on to them. They will return sooner if you aren't contracted by trying to hang on to them. Notice them and allow them to appear and disappear. Allow them to show up. Notice when you notice that they show up. Breathe and relax and let them all go. Then notice. Don't look for them. Just Notice.
39. **Fuzzy Awareness and Focus.** Doing this will help with the previous practice. Awareness is fuzzy. Let all

focus go from your awareness and watch the world from your peripheral vision. Then focus your eyes intently on an object, like a chair or a rock in front of you. Go back and forth between awareness and focus. Increase the speed of doing this more and more until they seem to combine. When they combine, then you will be able to do both at the same time. Possibility (fuzzy) offers you the choice and making the choice (focus) moves you forward. Awareness and focus experienced together at the same time give you increased energy and power.

40. **Bilocation.** Split your perception into two and see yourself in another place, like another room or on a chair across from you. If you believe you can't split your perception, then pretend or imagine you can. Perceive the world from this new location. What does it look like? Then turn to face your original self. When you have changed your perception, call all of yourselves back to you. Say, *I now call all of my selves back to me, clean, clear, and abundant.* If you don't call all yourselves back, you may feel thin and scattered.

41. **Entrain Your Energy to a Higher Energy like Peace, Love, or Joy**. Feel what those energies feel like. You can name an energy whatever you like. How do you entrain your energy to it? By asking the Universe to show you Joy and then by stepping into that Joy and hanging out there. You are simultaneously naming It and claiming it .

42. **Listen to Silence**. Look for the silence between the sounds of the birds, frogs, and crickets. Listen to the silence when the wind stops. Breathe in that silence. This will silence your mind and put you into spaciousness.
43. **Lucid Dreaming.** When you go to sleep tonight, ask to have a lucid dream. Look for your hands or your feet or some object. Relate to that object. Know that you are dreaming. Have an intention to do something in your dream. Once you realize that you are dreaming, then do that thing you intended to do. You can also ask to learn something. Once you realize you are dreaming, then ask to learn about what you want to learn.
44. **Fireworks in the Chakras.** Start at the bottom and open the root chakra and place in it a brilliant display of fireworks. It can be mostly reds here. Then work your way up through all the colors of the chakras: orange, yellow, green (or pink), blue, indigo, and violet. End with silver and gold fireworks. Feel the fireworks as they explode in your chakras. Be the energy of the fireworks as they are exploding. Don't forget to end with the finale of boom, boom!
45. **Dance of the Chakras.** Dance the tango with each of your chakras' energies. Each of the chakras receives more power when we dance. Approach and retreat. Approach and retreat. It is the tango. As you ask the heart chakra to follow you, ask it what energy it is, and then you give it more of your energy. You lead and it

follows. It leads and you follow. Back and forth. The energy increases as you dance with it. Do this with each of your chakras. Ask each chakra, *What energy are you?* And it will ask, *What energy are you?* And then you dance.

Chapter 8 Allow WOW: Energy of Joyfinity

46. **Laugh Your Chakras**. Start laughing into your belly. Simply notice the contraction. Then see if you can bring that same laughing contraction one chakra higher into your power chakra. Now move the laughing contraction up to your heart chakra. Turn *Ahh* into a laugh. Next go to your throat chakra. Start chuckling. Go to the third eye chakra. This will be a high-pitched giggle. Think of *e*. Now go to the crown chakra. The sound of this laughter is a chortle with a *hmm*. Now go back and give yourself a good belly laugh. What is that like?

47. **Jellyfish.** Inhale into your lower abdomen and then exhale down into the earth as far as you can go. Breathe into your belly from as high as you can reach into the heaven and then breathe out into the earth as far as you can go. Repeat by breathing up from the earth and releasing the breath into the heavens. Feel each breath and flip the direction of the breath at the belly. Feel the air as it carries the energy of spirit. Notice how the breath begins to breathe you like the movement of a jellyfish.

48. Universe Breathing. Place your hands beside your ears about a foot away. Face the palms in. Wait and listen and feel. You will feel a pulsing in your hands. This pulsing is the wave energy of the universe. It is the same rhythm as the universe breathing. Synchronize your breath with this pulsing.

49. The Roll of Enlivening. Roll the energy starting from your root chakra all the way up, contracting each area of each chakra and in between each chakra as you go. Exhaling as you do this. Then as you reach the top, sigh and exhale as you let it go. And then watch as the air rushes in through your crown and washes down your entire system.

Next engage your back in the process. Reverse the process and roll your back starting at the tailbone in an arch stretching up to your crown. Tilt your head back and let the energy go out your forehead and the top of your crown.

Then engage your sides. Started squeezing them in at the base and roll that squeeze on both sides together up to your head.

 Let love do the work.

Appendix

Morning Prayer

Saying my Morning Prayer is how I begin all my mornings. I have done so for many years. The formalization of this prayer began when I was in Bimini in the Bahamas, but there were many less formalized predecessors before then. This prayer was inspired by St. Francis of Assisi's prayer, "Let me be an instrument of thy peace."

I ask to be an instrument or a vessel. But my prayer goes beyond being a vessel, as I already know that I am one. I am really asking that I might notice how much I am a vessel in any given moment. And asking, *Is there even more than that?* My surroundings are just a reflection of the state I am in—so noticing them is just noticing myself.

Today's word is *Truth*. So how much truth do I see reflected back at me, and where do I see it? I think that the day is early, and we shall see.

Each word that I ask about is featured as one of the chapters in one of my two previous books plus a couple of new words in this book. To the previous words, I've added *Awareness* and *Purpose*. They are included in My Morning Prayer, which currently goes like this:

> *Thank you, God, for this beautiful day. Thank you. Thank you. Thank you for this wonderful place we live. Thank you for the plants and animals that share our lives with us. And today for the wonderful … fire in the fireplace. (Add your own words here. The more gratitude you show, the greater the response from the Universe.)*
>
> *Make me an instrument of thy peace, love, joy, beauty, harmony, grace, healing, communication, abundance, gratitude, magic, bliss, truth, divine perfection, co-creation, breath, caring, freedom, glory, intent, laughter, magnificence, magnitude, power, presence, purpose, awareness, wisdom, and wonder.*
>
> *What shall I notice today?*
>
> *What shall I be so much of that everything reflects it back to me; so much of that I stand in awe of my own being? I listen. And I hear, "Truth." Today my word is "Truth."*

I start with gratitude for the day and for all things. The deeper I go into gratitude, the greater the experience becomes. I know that all magic starts with the catalyst of gratitude, no matter what the day looks like. A gorgeous sunrise makes it easy to be thankful. So, I usually start there, because it is easy.

Often, it is rainy, cloudy, cold, or windy. I am still grateful. Today, it is four degrees below zero. I am grateful. I am grateful to be sitting in front of the fireplace, warmed by the glow of the embers, writing this book.

The Pivotal Joy Experience

 I don't have to bring in Joy. Just stop repressing it.

A Billion Sparkles of Joy

Sunrise over the Bimini Flats at the marina is spectacular. It would be impossible not to feel the magnificence. Fingers of pink, lavender, and gold touch the aqua sea. I am in such gratitude. I am thankful for being alive and for each breath of air. For the retreat I am attending. For the couch I sit on. For the sparkling water and the sunrise. I then ask God, "Show me how much Joy I can possibly be." How much Joy can God be through me? I wait. And then I am showered with a billion sparkles of light. I feel my body explode out into the universe as billions of sparkles of Joy. I wonder. Will I come back together again? Or will I remain a billion pieces of light out in the universe. I come back together. But then I wonder. Can I walk?

I was greeting the morning sunrise on February 15, 2016, in the Bahamas at Bimini and saying my Morning Prayer. At that time there were only Peace, Love, and Joy in my list of the aspects of God. The others were added later. When I got up to leave, I stood up and the ground not only supported me, but it giggled when I walked on it. Then I wondered if I could eat and swallow food. I went into the buffet at the hotel, and the food tasted exquisite. Even the water was exquisite. I ran up to people and said that I was so full of Joy that I couldn't contain it. They said, "Don't contain it." So, I didn't. I shared it. And I am still sharing it today. I can relive that experience any time I choose, although it is slightly different each time. I can simply go there and feel the exquisite Joy of the billion sparkles of light that I am.

Rikka Zimmerman's Six Principles

In the following representation of Rikka Zimmerman's Six Principles, I give gratitude for each principle.

a. Thank you for *everything being in love*.
b. Thank you for *being whole and complete*.
c. Thank you for *being fully supported by God*.
d. Thank you for *being seen and heard by God*.
e. Thank you for *infinite possibilities*.
f. Thank you for *everything already being done*.

The Rules of Energy

Rules of Energy

These are the rules of energy as printed in *Absolute Joy*.
1. Matter is a kind of dense energy. Some say contracted.
2. Energy flows.
3. Energy will not be contained.
4. Energy emanates from Source.
5. Source is everywhere and nowhere at the same time.

6. Matter is a reflection of the intent of Source.
7. Energy is inside of matter and outside of matter at the same time.
8. Flow requires time and space.
9. In the absence of time and space, nothing flows, and everything flows in all directions from all points at the same eternal moment.
10. Energy cannot be created or destroyed. It is eternal.

Resources

Online Resources

Leslie Sandra Black: www.heartawakening.ca

www.Healthlaboratorylive.com

Christine Laria: https:// christinelaria.com

Dr. Sue Morter: www.drsuemorter.com

Books

Dodd, Ray. *The Toltec Secret to Happiness*. Hampton Roads Publishing, 2003, 2014.

Dyer, Wayne. *Your Sacred Self*. HarperCollins, 1995.

———. *There's a Spiritual Solution to Every Problem*. HarperCollins, 2001

Morter, Dr. Sue. *The Energy Codes*. Atria Books, 2019.

Spalding, Baird T. *Life and Teaching of the Masters of the Far East*. 6 vols. DeVorss Publications, 1924-96.

Spiritual Practitioners

These are some of the spiritual practitioners that I quote or refer to in this book.

Leslie Sandra Black: Leslie is a bestselling author and founder of Heart Awakening.

Esther Hicks: Esther is an inspirational speaker and co-author of nine books. She has presented numerous workshops on the Law of Attraction. She appeared in the 2006 film, *The Secret*.

Nikole Kadel: Nikole is a facilitator of spiritual expansion. She leads mystical, dynamic excursions that allow people to connect with nature in such places as Bali and Tonga.

Christine Laria: Christine is a consciousness and awakening guide, sound healer, and certified life coach. Christine offers regular sound baths and intuitive guidance.

Dr. Sue Morter: Dr. Sue is the founder of the Morter Institute for BioEnergetics, speaker, and bestselling author of *The Energy Codes*.

Rikka Zimmerman: Rikka is a global leader in consciousness, the creator of Adventure in Oneness LLC. She is also a singer and songwriter. She utilizes unique toning techniques designed to shift the listener into a higher vibrational and energetic alignment.

About Tricia Jeane Croyle

Tricia Jeane Croyle is an architect and a Life Transformed Coach. Her life has centered on teaching, architecture, introspection, travel, storytelling, and horses.

Tricia received a BA from Macalester College in Minnesota, a BED in environmental design and architecture from the University of Minnesota, and an MOB in business from Silver Lake College in Wisconsin. She has spent a lifetime of inner awakening brought about by experiences in the Peace Corps; living and working in exotic places including Micronesia, Polynesia, Spain, and China; and traveling to sacred places such as Machu Picchu, Bimini, Sedona, Kona, and Nan Madol.

Through the years, she has made contributions to environmental protection, sustainable architecture, and education. She established Silver Creek Designs LLC as an architecture company specializing in sustainable and sacred architecture. She is the creator of *Joyfinity®*, an energetic system. She is an author, speaker, and life coach. She currently lives in Wisconsin with her husband of fifty-plus years, two cats, and six horses.

 I am the expert of nothing.

www.ingramcontent.com/pod-product-compliance
Lightning Source LLC
LaVergne TN
LVHW051559070426
835507LV00021B/2668